# Basic Questions
# of Life and Death

HERBERT WADDAMS

# Basic Questions
# of Life and Death

LONDON
EPWORTH PRESS

© HERBERT WADDAMS 1968
FIRST PUBLISHED IN 1968
BY EPWORTH PRESS
Book Steward: Frank H. Cumbers

SBN 7162 0038 4

PRINTED IN GREAT BRITAIN BY
CLARKE, DOBLE & BRENDON LTD
CATTEDOWN, PLYMOUTH

# Contents

These lectures were given in the hall of the St Albans College of Further Education at the invitation of the St Albans and District Council of Churches during Lent 1966. They were in part an attempt to express some of the ideas of Teilhard de Chardin.

Quotations from the following works are included by permission of the publishers:

Teilhard de Chardin, *The Future of Man* (Collins)
Teilhard de Chardin, *Hymn of the Universe* (Collins)
Teilhard de Chardin, *Le Milieu Divin* (Collins)
Claude Cuénot, *Teilhard de Chardin* (Burns & Oates)
Michael Ramsey, *Sacred and Secular* (Longmans Green)

# [1]

## *How is it possible to believe in God today?*

*Language about God*

OUTSIDE the main entrance to Westminster Abbey there is a shop belonging to the Abbey, which sells books. Some months ago someone who had been looking at the goods displayed in the window went in and protested about the title of one of the books which was prominently displayed. The title of the book in question was *God Is No More*.

It is not difficult to see why a visitor to Westminster Abbey should be taken aback by seeing such an announcement. Perhaps he had himself just come out from a service in the Abbey, where he had been singing Psalm 46—'God is our hope and strength' or the metrical version of Psalm 90 'O God our help in ages past'. On the face of it there is a rather startling contradiction to find God Is No More proclaimed in the bookshop which actually belongs to one of our best known buildings, set aside for the worship of God.

The book with this title was written by a clergyman of the Church of England and his wife, and it has been commended by Dr John Robinson, Bishop of Woolwich. In a recent book of his own the Bishop writes of the need to clear away false beliefs of what the Christian faith means, and he names this book as one of the two 'in which people have found greatest liberation' (*The New Reformation* p. 18).

The destruction of false ideas about Christianity has been one of the chief aims of Dr Robinson, and he evidently sees this book as an ally taking part in the same operation. The object of such writing is not, of course, merely negative. The authors see their task as the removal of what is false so as to give free course to what is true. Such an objective we must agree to be good, even though we may have reservations about the way in which it is done. It seems clear that one method which some of this school of writing follow is to use language which is aimed at riveting people's attention by a kind of shock treatment, and the title of the book in question falls into this category. When Dr Robinson's best seller *Honest to God* was first introduced to the British public, *The Observer* had banner headlines reading 'Our image of God must go'. Whether Dr Robinson had any responsibility for this phrase or not, it accords pretty well with the technique he himself often adopts. He tries to arouse Christians by shocking them out of what he considers to be their complacency with inadequate ideas about their religion.

We do not need now to examine an old dispute as to whether this is a good thing to do from a practical point of view. For, whether it is or not, the method has raised important points concerning the language we use about God and about the Christian faith. As we cannot communicate, either among ourselves or with other people, without the use of language, it is necessary to give some attention to this side of the matter before dealing with other things. It is possible that in the process of thinking about our language, other important truths concerning our subject as a whole will come to light.

We must begin by recognizing that words are only symbols of the things to which they refer. That is to say, they do not themselves present to our mind a picture of what they are trying to express. In the case of a photograph, for example, we see with our eyes something of the same thing which we should see if we were looking at the subject. There are differences, of course, but the point is that it is a representation of the thing as it is, as nearly as possible as it can be achieved: it is a picture.

We might try to *draw* a picture with the same object. But, if we try to describe something in words, we are engaged in quite a different process. Here the words are used to describe by referring to other things which we know and by comparing the object with these other things. The comparisons may be of different sorts—measurements, relationships, colours, other objects similar to that in question. In doing this we move within the experience of everyday life, and, because people have roughly similar experiences, they recognize the common measurements or comparisons which we use in order to convey our meaning.

If, however, we move beyond the attempt to describe something in merely physical terms, we find a further difficulty. We may perhaps have been impressed, even 'carried away', by the beauty of a sunset or of the mountains, and we want to convey this experience to a

9

friend. We can't do it merely by a physical description, unless indeed the friend has had so close an experience of his own that even the mention of the fact brings to him a remembrance of what he felt. The mere recitation of the colours of a sunset, or even the complete physical analysis of some building of great beauty, does not convey the beauty itself. To try to convey beauty in words involves using words which have been invented for the ordinary things of daily experience, or new words to do something much more difficult, namely to convey a spiritual or aesthetic experience.

We shall find that words are sadly inadequate to do what we want, unless we are poets, and then we shall use words themselves in a special evocative way. But if it is difficult to explain a fairly common experience of beauty by the use of words, it is bound to be even more difficult to speak of God adequately with words, for the experience which we have of him is spiritual, and by definition, if God is God, he is far beyond our thinking, and therefore immensely, infinitely, beyond words which do not meet even the needs of our own everyday experiences.

Does this mean then that it is no use speaking at all? Of course it does not, for words are the only means of communication available to us in such a case, and we have to use them. But it does mean something very important, and it is this: in speaking of God and the things of God our words are but pointers, symbols of the truth. They do not reach the truth, still less contain it, but they point men towards it, and enable them to make contact with it, if they desire to do so.

*Image and Symbol*

It is important to notice the difference between images on the one hand and symbols on the other. An image is a substitute for something or somebody: a symbol on the other hand is meant to point away from itself to something other. An image encloses something within itself, a symbol frees the seer or hearer to escape from itself into the thing to which it points.

When we come to speak of God, we must avoid the pitfall of making our symbols into images, for then they become idols.

This distinction is not made clear by Dr Robinson, for example, though much of what he has written has been aimed at escaping from images which imprison the idea of God within inadequate thought. To use his own words: 'But, as soon as they (sc. the images) become a substitute for God, as soon as they become God, so that what is not embodied in the image is excluded or denied, then we have a new idolatry, and once more the word of judgement has to fall. In the pagan world, it was—and still is—a matter, in the main of metal images. For us, it is a question much more of mental images—as one after another serves its purpose and has to go' (*Honest to God*, pp. 125-6).

What we have to notice here is that it is the image idea that makes these things wrong, not necessarily the use of words themselves, if they are understood as symbols, and are recognized as inadequate in themselves to express fully the truth to which they are pointing. The Bishop of Woolwich picks out one or two images of this kind: the two to which he seems most opposed are those of God 'up there' or 'out

11

there'. There are dozens of other symbols in the Bible, which are used to convey different aspects of God's work or nature. Picture language may be rightly used as a symbol, but not as an image.

One of the troubles in dealing with writers like Bishop Robinson is that they speak of the things they wish to condemn, as though all Christians except themselves use them in a crude and unintelligent way. There may in primitive societies have been those who believed literally that God was to be located spatially in the sky, but the number of people in our time who take this sort of simple attitude about the language they use is limited to the very young and the mental sub-normal. He is therefore, to a large extent, tilting at windmills, as far as God being 'up there' is concerned. Do we not use this kind of symbolic language every day of our lives without thinking twice about it? When we gladly tell our friends that our child has gone *up* into the next class, do we really think it necessary to explain that he did not float through the ceiling or climb the stairs, and that in fact the next class is taught two floors lower than that which he has just left? When we go *up* to town, are we in any doubt about what we mean? Are the *up* and *down* lines of the railway so difficult to understand? It is nonsense to suggest that the language which we use every day in a symbolic sense can not be used in parallel ways in our discussion about God.

This point is important, because alarm and despondency have been spread abroad among Christians, who now feel that they are guilty of all kinds of offences by the wrong use of language. This can have the effect of creating a sense of uncertainty about belief in God, and, even more, of inhibiting people from talking about God. That it has actually had this effect is, I believe, incontestable. This weakens Christian witness and Christian life.

It is a good thing that we should take notice of the dangers of the improper use of pictures, but, having done so, we should then feel more free than before to use symbols as a necessary means of conveying truth. We shall then guard against a misunderstanding of what these symbols are for. In a thorough examination of the whole question of the symbolism of height Dr Edwyn Bevan came to this conclusion (*Symbolism and Belief*, Beacon Press, Boston, 1957, p. 81):

'. . . when we look back upon the primitive tendency to regard the sky as the special domain of the Chief Being, we see it as a singularly apt anticipation of the truth. It expressed in a vivid way the feeling of the otherness of God: the sky was the other world removed from the accessible world round about man by distance in a third dimension; its distance when he looked up-wards gave him a feeling of the sublime which we can recognize as analogous to the feeling which, for us, is the ground tone of worship, the recognition of God's incomparable worth; in the phenomena of wind and lightning and thunder, primitive man saw a revelation of overwhelming power, and if Otto is right, no religion even to-day can dispense with an element akin to fear: in the higher starry regions primitive man saw the revelation of perfect order, unvarying law, and Christians to-day face the spiritual disorders of the world about them with the belief that there is a sphere of being in which there is no disharmony and no evil: "Thy will be done on earth as it is done in heaven".'

## Beyond and Within

There is one significant phrase here which we should do well to note. The use of height 'expressed in a vivid way the feeling of the otherness of God'. This is what is usually called the *transcendence* of God—that God is other than the world and man, beyond them, infinitely greater: whereas his close association with the world is known as his *immanence*. Dr Robinson wishes to abandon not only the idea of God 'up there' but also of God 'out there'. In urging us to escape from these ideas he is inevitably weakening the idea of the transcendence of God, the otherness of God, whether he means to do so or not, and this impression certainly comes over strongly in his book. So long as we bear in mind the cautions which we have already noted, then 'out there' can be as good a symbol as 'up there', if it expresses the fact that God is without as well as within the world.

Dr Robinson's wish is that these transcendent metaphors should be put aside in favour of another, that of depth. And here one can only say that he gives the impression of falling into the very trap which he wants to avoid for other people. If one adopts his way of expounding the ideal of ultimate depth, and God as the ground of our being, one seems in fact to be using depth as an image and not as a symbol, and in this case, instead of being a liberating influence, it must in the end be just as constricting as those of which he disapproves. To those who have a naturally strong sense of God's immanence, this new image will give a feeling of freedom, but it will be a false sense for it is just as bad to be imprisoned within one image as within another.

14

Moreover the course recommended by Dr Robinson is contradicted by his own principles. He has given excellent reasons why an image which uses spatial metaphors should be considered inhibiting. But, if what he says is true (though it is only true when these are used wrongly) then exactly the same objections apply to his own form of image. It is in fact on *his* showing merely the substitution of one picture to another: it may or may not be a more satisfactory or helpful picture, but on his own principles it is quite inadmissible.

But more serious than the question of whether this or that form of expression is to be used, is the general impression which Dr Robinson's book gives of confining knowledge of God to what man finds within himself. I put this in a rather sharp and exaggerated form so as to make the point clear. The book seems to be mainly concentrated on God as the ground of our being, with the result of encouraging men to look inwards rather than outwards in their search for God. This is a danger if not corrected. Like other aspects of his thought it has opportunities as well as dangers, and it is necessary to look at both. It is true that we must start from ourselves in our search for God, for we ourselves provide the only platform on which we can stand in that search. But it is necessary at the same time to beware of the risk of too easily identifying what we find in ourselves with God. When we begin the search it is vital that we should have a sense of the otherness of God strongly present in our minds, for otherwise he cannot be found.

There is another aspect of the otherness of God which we should not fail to note. It is clear that our thoughts and language may give a proper place to the otherness of God and at the same time omit one very important consideration. This is the fact that God is far beyond anything we can speak of or even think. If he were not, he would not be God at all. When we have done everything possible to point to the truth which we know about God, this truth is only a tiny fraction of the whole truth which is God. The use of the word 'beyond' to indicate this truth is not enough, as it may merely mean that God is not dependent on us, which is of course also true. We need also to be reminding ourselves constantly that there is a vast area of truth about God of which we know absolutely nothing because our finite minds cannot go further than the outer fringes of the reality of God.

This does not make our knowledge of God any less reliable or any less true, but it enables us to see our own limitations in speaking of it. It also helps us to realize that to know our own limitations is a necessary part of seeing truth in proportion. If we think that we are able to comprehend all the truth, it produces in us quite a different attitude of mind from our attitude when we know that it is only a small part of the whole. Intellectual humility is important in our search for truth, and, like other forms of pride, intellectual pride causes us to see things in the wrong perspective.

*Myth*

Perhaps at this point we ought to notice the use of a word which is often confusing, and that is the word 'myth'. It has several quite distinct meanings, and unless we appreciate this we shall often be misled. 'Myth' can be and often is used in popular language as meaning something which is untrue: this corresponds to the

16

meaning given in the dictionary as 'figment'. The curious thing about this meaning is that it is exactly the opposite of what 'myth' means in its other sense, namely, a story which conveys truth through the thought forms of its day. In this it is very like the meaning of symbol, which we have already discussed. 'Myth' in this sense is particularly important to religion just because it is impossible to describe religious truth in ordinary language: a story therefore is used to convey this truth.

In some things we have become so literal minded in our use of language that we often ask the wrong questions about a statement. We do not ask first what it is meant to say to us. Instead we ask whether the outward details of the story correspond to facts which can be outwardly measured. The Old Testament provides many examples of this. History, in our way of looking at it, is often concerned with small details of fact: for example, we spend an immense amount of time and attention in trying to answer the question whether it was at three o'clock or at four o'clock that something happened. I am not saying that this is unimportant, or that we should not try to find out the facts, but merely pointing out a way of looking at things which is different for us than for many of our forefathers.

Their view of history was not concerned with whether the facts were accurate but with the meaning of the events which underlay them. The Jews particularly were more concerned with the message than with the details. We could say that they were concerned with truth rather than with facts. If we take the deliverance from Egypt as an example, it was the truth that God delivered them from the Egyptians which really

17

mattered, not whether the description of the plagues was in every case historically accurate and correctly explained. And any person with a sense of balance must, I think, agree that they put the stress on what was most important. The details are now relatively insignificant, whereas whether their deliverance was the act of God is still a living question affecting their daily life and outlook.

When people are trying to convey a truth, they have to use the language and the concepts with which they are familiar. If they believe in a three-storied universe, which is the usual illustration chosen for this purpose, then they will talk in terms of a three-storied universe, and they have to talk in this way 'to get their message across'. But these terms and thought forms are only the outer clothing of the idea which they are trying to convey. We must not suppose that it is the real content and, if we mistake the husk for the kernel, we shall not be able to understand what we are trying to study. The truth has to be disentangled from the outer clothing in which it is presented and put into terms which we now understand and which are familiar to us. That is our form of myth. Every generation clothes truth in its own kind of clothes—it is the clothes which form the myth: the truth is to be found inside them. We have to find out the truth of an out of date kind of myth and put it into our own kind of myth. The first activity is called 'demythologizing', and is rather a favourite with some theologians.

If someone says that the Bible is full of myth, we can all readily agree and point out that it is the only way there is in which to convey truth, and that we only learn many important things today by using twentieth century myths. So too, as we have seen, in writing

18

history it is merely absurd for us to expect ancient writers to have had the same attitude as we have today. Theirs was in some ways a fuller and richer approach than our rather desiccated attitude.

Another point of which we should be conscious is the fact that many of the problems which people think to be modern problems are not really modern at all. It is, I suppose, a natural temptation to all of us to imagine that the particular difficulty or aspect of religion with which we are concerned is something which we have discovered for ourselves. But it is a serious error to suppose, because we have only just thought of it, that no one else before us has done so. Some of the writers of our day seem to fall into the trap of thinking that their own problems are quite new, whereas in fact they are thinly disguised problems which have occurred at various periods of the Church's history. Our knowledge of nature is immensely greater than that of the past, but this does not in itself make a difference to the basic questions about human existence which underlie the life of men.

*Relation of the World to God*

In the early centuries of the Church there was a strong movement which concentrated on the human side of the world's meaning and underestimated or ignored the divine. The tendency of this thinking was to separate the earthly from the heavenly so that there was no really effective link between them. This was a tendency which came from Greek thinking and was imported from there into the thinking of some Christians. It is not always easy to keep the right

19

balance between the human and divine, but the Christians of the early centuries saw clearly that unless this link was a real and living bond, then the essence of the Christian Gospel would be lost.

The belief which gives expression to this link is that of the incarnation of Christ, viz., that God entered this world and united himself with mankind in the person of Jesus Christ, in whom we see both the divine and the human elements perfected within the conditions of his life and time. Today there can be found in the writing of some authors tendencies which could easily lead to the same kind of separation, and, if they did so, they too would undermine the Christian Gospel. The authors in most cases deny that they intend this; nevertheless the logic and influence of their approach may in fact have this result.

It is, of course, true that our understanding of God is mediated through our own experience. We can never get away from this fact. It is we who know things, it is we who experience things. But there is a subtle difference between experiencing something which acts upon us from outside, coming into our own life, and something which is contained within ourselves. If we concentrate all our attention on ourselves and on the world immediately around us, we may confine ourselves to that world without meaning to do so, and we may see our experience in the wrong perspective, just because we have not taken into account the possibility of its relation to other reality than our own selves.

Everything in the world is related to Jesus Christ. We say in the creed that it is through the Word of God that all things were made, a belief which comes directly from the first chapter of St. John's Gospel. And it is indeed only in Christ that the world and everything in it is being remade and renewed, for it has been deeply affected in its meaning and its possibilities through the death and resurrection of Jesus Christ. To understand this we must have a deep appreciation of the fact that God has intervened in Jesus Christ from *outside* our own normal processes. If we dissect and examine everything within our own natural processes, we can discover many useful things, but we can never get from such an examination the vital truths of God's action in saving the world.

The modern writers to whom I have referred often confine their attentions to the world, as though out of that could be distilled its own salvation, if only we can find the key or look at it in the right way. This is a delusion and it brings back in our time the separation between earth and heaven, between the human and divine, which threatened to lead Christians astray in earlier ages. This tendency seems to be associated with the claim that man has 'come of age', and it results in what may rightly be called secularization—that is, an interest in this world alone, the concept that there is nothing outside this world that is relevant to the fulfilment of man. Coming from the Latin word 'saecula' meaning world, secularization aptly describes this attitude.

A recent line favoured by the avant-garde writers of theology is to insist that we have to secularize our Gospel. This is a confusing way of putting it, for the word 'secularization' can bear, as we have just noted, a meaning which is entirely unChristian, meaning a concentration on the world which excludes God. The use of these words often follows fashions: the latest cliché is taken up as a sign that we are 'with it' theologically. Unfortunately too often those who use them do not always define what they mean: and one suspects sometimes that they do not know themselves!

'Secularization' is the latest of these fashionable up-to-date words. Its ordinary and proper meaning is bad, but it is used by some writers to mean something good. So far as I can follow them (for example Harvey Cox in his book *The Secular City*), they mean by the word that the Church has to be relevant to the world as it is —a notion which, when put like that, is not as new as they would like it to sound. To bring it home to people and to make it sound new, they use words like 'secular' to carry a meaning which has hitherto been uncommon, but which it can bear if carefully explained. The Archbishop of Canterbury has recently written a well balanced little book called *Sacred and Secular*, in which he sets out the right relationship between the two.

There is one valuable side of this presentation of which Christians ought to take particular notice, for it shows how great a gap exists between them and the world outside. You have only to hear the kind of questions about the Christian faith which are put in the Forces on such occasions as Padre's Hours to realize the total ignorance which prevails among many people. And this is not merely an ignorance of facts, as, for example, we might be ignorant of the way in which newspapers are produced. It goes far deeper than this, and reveals that the majority of our fellow countrymen today move in quite another thought world from that of the Christian faith. In this sense their outlook is secularized. They have no room for a world outlook which includes God. God for them has become an unnecessary addition which merely complicates their life as they see it.

This is made difficult to deal with because the ideas

which the word 'God' conveys to them have almost nothing in common with what Christians, who understand their Gospel, really believe. It is usually compounded of a number of crude elements, in which perhaps the chief constituents are Old Testament ideas culled from Bible stories learnt before they left Sunday school at the age of eight (though far fewer go to Sunday school at all now), together with inadequate stories of the same kind which they have picked up in the so-called religious instruction periods at school, plus pictures of God which appear in old paintings or illustrations in nineteenth century Bibles. It is perhaps worth noting too that some of our present day authors encourage them in their ideas of what Christians teach by the technique which they employ of 'guying' other people's views in order to establish their own. It is the well known 'Aunt Sally' method of putting up something which they know they can knock down.

The net result is that when such words as 'God' and other traditional phrases are used, they often convey to the outsider ideas which Christians strongly disapprove of. Great caution has to be exercised in speaking to others, so as not to ingrain in their minds wrong views, which must be rooted out before they can know the truth. In other words we have to rid their minds of the wrong kinds of ideas which they have associated with the thought of God.

This is going to be a long business. It means that we ourselves have to adopt a strict and hard discipline in examining our own thought and the way we express things. We must also listen carefully to what non-Christians say, not because we are going to agree with them, but because, unless we listen carefully to what they say, we shall not be able to learn what language they are using, and what exactly is at the back of their minds when they use words which are familiar to us, but which for them carry quite another meaning. If we do not understand their language, we shall not be able to communicate with them by words at all, and this will be a serious obstacle in bringing them to the truth.

The importance of this was stressed at the British Faith and Order Conference at Nottingham in September 1964. The section dealing with the subject of faith reported: 'The world is asking profound questions concerning itself. We too are affected by the restless searching for meaning and purpose in life exemplified in much of contemporary literature and art. If we are to understand our faith in God, and make that faith meaningful to our contemporaries, we must face these questions in their contemporary form. We must allow the world to put its questions to us in its own terms, for it is God's world despite the distortions of sin' (p. 59).

The section also stressed the vital importance of Christians facing these issues together. It said 'Our faith requires that we face honestly the questions which the world poses, and that together we resolutely seek a visible unity which matches the unity we already hold in faith.'

You will have noticed that besides the need for communicating with others, there is another reason why we should listen carefully to the questions of outsiders. 'If we are to understand *our* faith in God . . . we must face these questions in their contemporary form.' How can this be so? Surely we are not going to learn about our own faith by hearing the views of unbelievers? But the truth is that this is just the way in which our grasp of our own faith *is* going to be increased. The reason is simple when we see it. The faith which we know is a faith to help men find their true fulfilment and relation to God. Its purpose is to meet their need. The implications of our faith for that need can only be found when we really know the need—from inside. We have really to enter in to the inner attitudes of others, to 'sit where they sit', if we are to know what their needs are: that means we have to enter sympathetically into their difficulties. As we learn them, we find to our amazement and wonder that the Gospel, which perhaps we have been content to take as it came to us, is immensely richer and deeper than we thought, and, when this discovery is made, not only are we able to help the other person but we receive a great benefit ourselves.

But then comes the question as to how we can speak usefully to anyone about God, if the whole idea of God is clouded by wrong associations. Part of the answer to this is for us to remember that any statement about God is also by implication, a statement about the world and about man. It is, of course, possible to say something about God which does not in those words include anything about man, for example, that God is almighty. Any statement about the nature of God has inescapable corollaries which concern the world and man, and if we say that God is almighty, we inevitably also say that God is in his own life and existence independent of the world as a source: we say that he is not enclosed in the world or dependent upon it for his own power. This also means that man must be dependent upon God, and that the world can only take on meaning in relation to its maker. There are other derivative truths which spring out of such a statement about God, or out of any other such statement.

The most obvious example is the statement that God is love. It is not necessary to spell out how such a state-

25

ment as this affects the whole meaning of the world and of the life of man, for it is the heart of the Christian Gospel.

Nevertheless outsiders often have the impression that Christians are playing a sort of private game when they discuss the nature of God. They don't mind us playing the game, if we like that kind of thing, but it does not seem to them to have anything to do with human life in general or with their lives in particular. This is especially the case when they hear Christians speaking about doctrines like that of the Holy Trinity. The impression which they receive is partly due to the fact that Christians themselves have ceased to see how these teachings are relevant to their *own* lives. Christians must relearn that these beliefs are directly related to the possibility of understanding deeply what their day to day lives are.

We must never give the impression that God is an abstract, rather than a living God. It seems rather obvious to say that he has to be seen to be a God who has to do with us and with other people, but it is a sad fact that much of our time is spent in trying to speak to others of a God who is not related to their personal situation and condition. It is here that the writers of whom we have been critical, have something important to tell us. Our belief must have relevance to the life which our hearers are leading, if it is to convey anything useful to them. And this means that we have to be specially watchful not to allow ourselves to talk in terms which may be misunderstood, even in the use of the word GOD.

Christians are conscious of the reality of God in their lives and can speak of this among themselves, and be understood and helped. The outside world sees no connection between the lives its members lead and the God about whom we talk among ourselves. We have to translate all our statements about God into terms of living reality for those who need Him, but cannot find Him just because He is not related to their lives, so far as they can see at the moment.

Every statement about God then is a statement about man. It is not merely a question of putting our principles into practical form, so that we show in our lives what we mean by our professions of belief. That of course is most important, and it is a commonplace, on which we do not need to dwell, that Christians must commend their Gospel to the world by their own actions, their self-sacrifice, their love, and the depth of their living. But that is not our subject just now. We have to be able to show men that our statements about God have meaning for their own experiences, their own hopes and fears. The quotation from the Nottingham conference referred twice to 'meaning', and this is significant enough for us to note carefully. The report said 'We too are affected by the restless searching for meaning and purpose in life . . .' and then spoke of making our faith 'meaningful to our contemporaries'.

If this is correct, it implies that there is something about life which can be made meaningful—that those outside the Christian faith are dissatisfied with the absence of meaning, because they have some experience or conviction within themselves that there are things in their lives which *need* meaning; they feel that there is something deeper and more significant about their lives than is met merely by not bothering about ultimate meaning. If this is the case, it is a very important fact, and provides a starting point for Christians in trying to meet them.

27

## Divine Dimension

How can we describe the kind of meaning which we ourselves have known and which we want to pass on to others? We must be careful not to claim too much, or to recommend the Christian faith for the wrong reasons, for, if we do, when people find out, they will react even more strongly against listening in the future to anyone who claims to be Christian. Can we not say that the meaning of life can be described as a sense of the divine dimension? We know quite well that we can only see the wood when we stand back from the trees, and that to know the relation of things to other things outside themselves is vital for a sense of perspective and proportion. It is even more vital in matters which concern ultimate truth, and it is only when our lives are related to the divine dimension that they can be seen in their right perspective and true relations to other people and to the world.

We must therefore start with others—and perhaps we should do well to go back to the same place ourselves—from the experiences which men have of the mysteries of life, and I would say of the mysteries of love above all. For love, when it is true, is always partly a reflection of the author of all love, and is the best source of a beginning to understand God. I mention love because it is something of which every person has some experience, even if it is only at second hand by seeing it in other people. There are also other mysteries which arouse the sense of wonder in man, and I think it would be true to say that the most percipient scientists are aware of this sense of mystery and wonder, which comes to them through their own investigations.

This sense of wonder and mystery has nothing in common with an unsolved mathematical problem, or with the puzzlement which can be aroused in us by a skilful conjuror: it has quite another character. It is closer to the sense of beauty aroused by great music, or great painting, or by the beauties of nature. The mystery of beauty is impossible to explain factually. Indeed the more it is analysed the less there remains of it, and a beautiful building can only be measured in those things which leave its beauty completely unexplained.

The French priest Teilhard de Chardin, who died in 1955, was a trained palaeontologist and geologist as well as a theologian (that is a student of the oldest forms of life as revealed by fossils and of the strata in which they are found). He had insights, which may give us help in our problems of new understandings of how the truth of God may be better understood by our generation. He was convinced that modern man does have a sense of the divine within the world, a sense of the immanence of God, which is connected with the whole development of modern science. He produced a number of theories which were calculated to bridge the gap between the scientists' way of looking at things on the one hand and that of religious people on the other.

This is not the place to discuss the supposed conflict between science and religion, but we as Christians have to recognize very clearly the gap between the way many Christians think and the way scientists think. Of course it is possible to find people on both sides among whom such a gap does not exist, but the great majority of people are divided in the cast of their thinking, in the way they approach problems. We must also realize that many Christians have been content for too long merely to repeat the language which they learnt when they

29

were young, and consequently—as we have already suggested—they are found to be talking in thought forms which no longer communicate with those who have not had that same upbringing—or conditioning.

Teilhard de Chardin did much to bridge this gap as he belonged both to the scientific and to the religious world. He did not produce a system which would answer all questions, and there are still problems connected with his approach where it is not fully developed or related to the rest of experience. But he had many illuminating lines of thought, some of which can help us in our thought about the world and its relation to its creator.

Two in particular may be mentioned. One is his concept of matter and the other his idea of evolution: both are part of the same way of looking at the world. Let us take the second first.

To Teilhard evolution was the key to the understanding of the world, but he felt the normal use of the word 'evolution' to be inadequate to the reality of the world as he saw it as a result of his study of palaeontology. To most people evolution means that man has developed from the lower animals over a long process of time. This is certainly part of evolution, but to confine our idea of evolution merely to this section of the world and of time seemed to Teilhard to get everything out of proportion. Moreover, to isolate this little bit of the universe, namely that portion from the lower animals to man, is to take man out of the universe in our minds and to isolate him in an improper way. In other words we cannot speak or think of man by himself when we think of evolution, for it is only by seeing man in the whole setting that we can make sense of the universe.

Another common attitude is to think of man as being in some way 'finished'. We see man as starting from some form of lower animal and then gradually developing until he reaches the fully grown condition in which he now is. But there is no reason at all why man today should be the finished product. He may in fact be only half way, or a quarter way along the line of evolution, and the future may hold developments of which we have never dreamed. This is not to deny, of course, that man is the highest point which evolution has yet reached. This must be recognized, and indeed it is because of certain special characteristics of man that he now has responsibility for the way in which evolution will proceed in the future.

Teilhard de Chardin looked on man as one part of the whole pattern of evolution, which included the most ancient periods of the world's history, going back for millions of years. Man belongs intrinsically to that universe, and neither the universe nor man can properly be understood out of relation to one another.

He expressed dismay that evolution was still identified with biological evolution as propounded by Darwin, whereas it could only be understood in a universal setting. Darwinism concerned merely one branch of one part of the universe.

Darwin, as we know, introduced the theory of biological evolution which is generally accepted today. Teilhard's thought stretched much further and included in his evolutionary perspective the whole development of the universe from its first origin. He protests against the constricting effect of only seeing evolution in terms of biological development, that is in terms of the development of life.

When he views the universe as all part of one

immense evolution, this has consequences for our religious thought. Sometimes we hear complaints that some people have not caught up with post-Darwinian thought, viz., that they have not come to terms with the insights of Darwin and what has followed from them. But we do not wish to find ourselves enmeshed in post-Darwinian thought when that has itself become out of date. It is to escape the prison of inadequate ideas of evolution in Darwinian terms that Teilhard is urging us.

We have to see God as totally concerned with the developing evolution of the world, not only in the past but in the future. The universe is incomplete, and the development of man within it is incomplete also. This means that God is active and living in this continuing development, which is to come to a climax or fulfilment in the future. This brings back into current thought the element in the New Testament of what is still-to-come in the future of the world. God remains greater than the world and to a certain extent independent of it, but he is engaged in the working out within the world of the evolution which gives meaning to the world's past, present, and future. This must also involve the truth that God is intimately associated with the world in its struggle to realize its own potentialities: this is what the incarnation of Christ tells us. Thus we see that the making of the world, the redeeming of the world, the future of the world, are not isolated parts of the history of the universe, but are all aspects of the one, ever-active, work of God in close identification with the universe, as day by day the universe continues to be created, saved, and shaped for the future.

When we see the universe in this light we can hardly avoid the strong impression of a purpose running all through its development. How else can the extra-ordinary facts be reasonably accounted for? In this light the developments which are taking place are not merely changes from one thing to another, in a way which might in the end lead to the whole thing peter-ing out in meaningless dissipation, like a river dis-appearing into the sands of a vast delta: they are on the contrary a movement towards a new understanding of unity, in which the whole universe will be incorpor-ated, with man as its leading point.

These points may be expanded a little so as to draw out their meaning, as they throw light on our own atti-tudes and the way they should be changed. We have for hundreds of years been in the habit of thinking of creation as something which once happened and then —so to speak—was done. This static approach is deeply embedded in our thinking and we may find it difficult to abandon it. But there is nothing in it which is really necessary. If we consider the matter, we can see that, if we believe in a living and active God who is all the time penetrating our own lives and the life of the world, there is every reason to suppose that his activity—which is always a creative activity—is constantly being exercised. Therefore the static idea is basically wrong. God did not once create the world and then stop: he is now, and always has been, creating the world, and we partake in this moving and expanding universe which he is creating.

A reference to the book of Genesis is interesting, for there can be seen evidence for the new view rather than for the old. The story of Genesis is expressed in a partly static form, which is the reflection of the atti-tude of those who passed it down to us, but it contains within it this other dynamic element in the importance given to the succession of days, the means by which creation took place. And it is not difficult to go rather further than this, and to say that the very idea of days is that of a recurring pattern, and not of something which happened once for all and then stopped. If we put aside the way we are accustomed to read Genesis and read it in this new way, we can see that it can contain within itself the material for this more dynamic meaning. It is not suggested that our insight into the nature of the world should depend on the book of Genesis, but it is interesting to observe that the Biblical account of creation can bear another emphasis, if we are ready to look for it.

Men could not see God as the God of total evolution until they had been able to see the world as a 'cosmo-genesis', that is, as a universe which is still evolving. Although we know that God is transcendent, beyond the universe and not enclosed within it, we must not see the relationship between them as one which prevails between a worker and his work. The worker does his work and then it is done, and it is something separate from himself and something that, when done, is finished. God is much more involved in the world than that: he is closely linked with it by reason of the fact that it goes only by his creative activity.

Cosmogenesis is not just change. Evolution in Teilhard's sense, evolution of the whole universe is not a haphazard affair which may go anywhere and which merely goes in some direction or other accidentally. Cosmogenesis is evolution with a purpose, evolution which is progressing according to a plan, and Teilhard's view was that it is a development towards unity, or convergence in itself and with God.

Teilhard de Chardin brings what has been thought of

as the sacred into relation with the secular in a new way. The Archbishop of Canterbury, Dr Michael Ramsey, has written:

'I believe that Christians are called to something harder than a Christian mind in apartness from and in contrast with the secular mind. Rather are they called to a Christian mind which is utterly involved with the secular situations in which Christians live and can think Christian-wise in and through those situations. "The mind of Christ", which St Paul exhorts Christians to have, is the mind of the servant who emptied himself (Philippians: 2). Is it not a part of this mind not only to perceive divine truths which are utterly contrary to the world but also to perceive within the world, even in its unpromising aspects, signs of the presence and action of God and traces of his laws?' (*Sacred and Secular*, p. 61).

To this question we must answer with a hearty 'yes', though perhaps the word 'laws' sounds rather too static, as though God has drawn up a code which we have to investigate, and which sits there, so to speak, ready for us to analyse. But this is not what the Archbishop meant. God's laws are the pattern of God's action, unfolding before us as we examine the universe through scientific investigation and enquiry. As the grandeur of the pattern is exposed to our eyes, we can learn there new understanding of God and of his ways which can appeal more directly to our present generation, who are themselves both enjoying and pursuing knowledge with the material and the means which God has given to man.

# [2]

## Is there a key to the meaning of the universe?

IF WE ASK the question 'Is there a key to the meaning of the universe?' we assume that there is an answer, even if that answer is 'No'. But we assume more than that, because the form of the question itself contains ideas which we ourselves, in asking the question, think to have meaning. In other words we think it reasonable to talk of the possibility of meaning in the universe, or we should not have put the question in that form. The fact that we have an idea that there might be meaning in itself shows that we have a bias in favour of finding it. This is natural enough in Christians, whose answer is a foregone conclusion. But it seems to me to have another importance too.

When the Nottingham report of the British Conference on Faith and Order said that secular man was asking questions about whether life has a meaning or not, and if so, what it is, the Conference may of course have been mistaken. It may have been an idea cooked up in the minds of those who wrote the report, although I do not think so. In drawing attention to the questions of the world, it was, I believe, reporting an observed fact. Men do ask and are asking questions about meaning. Indeed they are asking the very question which is the title of this chapter, perhaps not in exactly the same form as the title, but in some form or other which raises essentially the same point.

We ought not to overlook the significance of this fact. Men who are unaware of the teaching of the Christian faith, or who are aware of it and have not accepted it, are asking questions of this kind, and, in doing so, to some extent may presuppose that the answer will be 'Yes'. You cannot have the idea of meaning unless it actually exists. If there were no meaning in life, then we could hardly discuss meaning in any useful sense at all, since we should have no experience of it, and the word 'meaning' would be a meaningless sound. But we know meaning in our own experience, because we impose it ourselves on the things which we do, and we know that it is to be discerned in the pattern of things which other people do.

One could go on to say that our experience of meaning is much wider than what we know in the actions and plans of individual people: in some sense the whole of modern science is based on some kind of meaning, even if the sense of it is strictly limited. If the relation of one thing to another did not cohere in an overall pattern, it would be impossible to investigate anything systematically, and science as we know it today would not and could not exist.

But this sense of meaning in science is limited to the area of investigation itself: it is a self-contained pattern

37

or interrelationship, and it means something only within that complete relationship: it does not tell us anything about whether there is some further meaning or purpose which governs the pattern from beyond itself, what we might call some transcendent meaning.

Indeed science excludes anything outside from influencing the pattern, because that would introduce a principle of uncertainty which would frustrate the value of the work of investigation which is undertaken. We have in fact found that there *is* a pattern, and in this sense a meaning, within the world of scientific enquiry. This does not carry the consequence that it has any purpose beyond itself however. We see then that the word 'meaning' can have two senses: one is the relationship of one thing to another within a defined sphere. For example if we are investigating the effect of cold upon the human body, we might observe some symptom, and not being sure whether or not it had any relevance to the investigation we are pursuing, we might properly say 'I wonder whether that has any meaning', by which we would intend to ask whether it had any relevance to the matter in hand.

The other sense in which the word is used is that of 'purpose'. This is also a common use. What did you mean to do when you did so and so? would be another way of saying What did you intend to do? What was your purpose? It is in this sense that our original question is formed. A 'key to the meaning of the universe' must mean something which makes sense of the whole by interpreting its purpose, if it has one.

Does the universe have some purpose, some meaning, which is beyond itself, transcendent in relation to itself? I think that this is certainly what was intended by the Nottingham report, when it referred to the

questions being asked by the world. And it is sugges-
tive that those who ask the question must, by asking
it, believe that an affirmative answer is both possible
and likely. People who ask the question at all are those
who feel the need for meaning in their own lives, and
their need is some sort of evidence that it can be satis-
fied. It is certainly far short of proof, but it is at least
a pointer. It is difficult to see how such a need could
have arisen, unless it was a response in some sense to
the fact that it is possible to satisfy it.

The question about meaning in the universe is the
other part of the general question of belief in God. If
it is possible to believe in God, it is important to know
what kind of God it is in which we can believe. And
the problem of meaning in the universe is the same
problem as the nature of the God in whom we are to
believe. Those then who do not formally accept belief
in God in any Christian sense, but who are seeking for
meaning in the universe, are paying an inadequate but
real and silent witness to the possibility of such a
God.

To the question 'Is there a key to the meaning of the
universe?' we answer—'Yes, the key is Christ'. Having
done so, we must go on to try to show how Christ
answers the various needs of those who seek the truth,
and we must beware of the temptation, the danger of
which we have already noted, to present Christ to those
who are outside in terms which, though familiar enough
to us, are either without content or have the wrong
content for them. And we also have to face the fact
that although our answer may be clear enough to us,
and although we may indeed present powerful reasons
for its acceptance by others, it cannot become their
answer merely by the process of argumentation or

reasoning. Before its full import can be appreciated it
has to be accepted in an inner conviction by commitment.

Let us return to some of the ideas which we were
earlier considering from Teilhard de Chardin. We saw
how he introduced a larger concept of evolution as a
process in which we are now still partaking, and which
includes the whole development of the universe from
the beginning in the long distant past until its final
consummation in the future. Man is destined to play
a vital-part in this development, as we shall see
later.

One feature of his presentation of these ideas was
his view of matter as something, not opposed to spiritual, but inherently spiritual in its own nature. This is
an integral part of his way of looking at the universe,
and like many of his insights opens new possibilities
in our own approach. Many people have been
accustomed to thinking of matter and spirit as being
opposed to one another. Indeed they have often made
this opposition the very basis of their religious thought.
We cannot deny that the idea of matter as somehow
evil, or at least an obstacle to the spiritual, has found
plenty of supporters in Christian history.

The fact that it is still sometimes held today can be
seen in the way in which many Christians still talk of
the material, as though there were something intrinsically wrong with it. Indeed you may even find people
who would define the words by opposing them to each
other. That is to say, if asked what 'spiritual' means,
they would say that it is something which is not
material: and on the other hand would define material
as something which was not spiritual. Such ideas are
catastrophic and carry hidden within themselves here-

sies against which the Church has often waged war. For we must be clear that in Christian teaching it has never been accepted that matter in itself is bad, or that of itself it is an obstacle to the Christian life.

The opposite is the truth. The material is part of the whole world: it is part of ourselves in our physical bodies, and without it we are not human beings at all. God saw everything he had made, as we read in Genesis, and he found it to be very good. The material is part of the very good things which God made. The proper idea of the spiritual is not that it is some kind of different 'thing' from the material, but that it is the material when it is permeated with and controlled by the Spirit of God. Of course we are all rather gross thinkers, being human and not always good specimens of the human. So we tend to think of spirit as a kind of 'stuff' in itself: we should be hard put to it perhaps to describe exactly what we do think, but often we make in our minds a kind of 'material' spirit, by picturing it as smoke or something of the sort. I don't want to put the point too crudely, but to sound a warning against a tendency which most of us have.

We have minds which are accustomed to think in more or less solid terms, and it is very difficult for them to think in any other. But, when considering the spiritual, we should do well to see it, not as something which is floating about on its own, but—so far as the world is concerned—as something material which is governed by a purpose. This does not answer all the questions which arise, and I put it forward simply as a means of counteracting what may be an inadequate habit of thought, which is too easily allowed to creep in.

Teilhard de Chardin wrote a 'Hymn to Matter' in

order to express his own deep conviction. He saw matter, as it came before him in his palaeontological studies over millions of years, as the womb of all that is good and spiritual in the universe of today. He looked upon the universe as one integrally developing whole, which began with matter and gradually grew into a more and more complex and spiritual condition. He did not, as we often do, have a picture of a material universe or world, existing by some means or other, and then man—the spiritual being—added to it as an extra, so to say. Man is the gradual outcome of what was there before and is himself part of that earlier material condition from which he sprang. I suppose one could say that his idea is that the ancestors of men were not merely the lower animals, but the original gases out of which the world came to birth, long before life was known.

Here again it can be argued that Teilhard is nearer to the underlying truths of the book of Genesis than our normal ways of looking at things have been. For the succession of events in those first chapters of the Bible show a continuous process beginning from chaos and going on uninterruptedly until man, if we do not allow our views of the story to be too much dictated by what might be called the anthropomorphic elements in the story, that is by the passages that picture God as talking to himself like a man, and saying to himself —'Let's see. What shall I do next?'

Listen to these words from the 'Hymn to Matter' (*Hymn of the Universe*, p. 69):

'I bless you, matter, and you I acclaim: not as the pontiffs of science or the moralizing preachers depict you, debased, disfigured—a mass of brute forces and base appetites—but as you reveal yourself to me today, *in your totality and your true nature.*

'I acclaim you as the universal power which brings together and unites, through which the multitudinous monads are bound together and in which they all converge on the way of the spirit.

'I acclaim you as the melodious fountain of water whence spring the souls of men and as the limpid crystal whereof is fashioned the new Jerusalem.

'I acclaim you as the divine *milieu*, charged with creative power, as the ocean stirred by the Spirit, as the clay moulded and infused with life by the incarnate Word.'

He wrote these words as part of a short story, but they were his own sentiments which he was expressing. You may think that this is more like a poem than a theological or factual statement, and so it is. But when we are dealing with the inner nature of reality itself, it is the poets and mystics who see through the outer shell into the inner meaning.

And Teilhard's view of matter and evolution is directly linked to Christ, for he sees in the incarnation of the Word of God in Christ the event which gives meaning to everything else. And, if we approach the subject with the light which he provides, we can find through it a richer and fuller understanding of what the incarnation means in the whole history of the world, past, present, and to come. For in Christ we see, concentrated in a point, in the life of one man, what God is doing in the universe; his purpose for the world; his own way of working and therefore his own nature; and how we as men are linked up with him in the whole process in which God himself is actively involved.

When we bring forward Christ as the key to the

universe, we do not do so because he is an inevitable conclusion reached by rational forms of argument, for it is clear that there are many rational men who do not reach this conclusion. There is a gap to be crossed, and though reason can bring men to the edge, the next step has to be taken by choice independent of conclusive reasoning, by faith.

There is a strong tradition, especially in Protestant theology of the last two hundred years, that it is no good thinking that we can find out anything about God by studying the world. It does nothing, according to this view, except land you with a false idea of what God is or could be. But I cannot myself accept this attitude, which is a departure from what Christian thinkers have thought through the centuries, and it also seems to me to be at variance with what we read in the Bible. It is certainly far removed from the Old Testament, where the Psalms are full of the glory of God in nature—'The heavens declare the glory of God and the firmament showeth his handiwork' (Psalms 19:1). Nor does it fit in with what we read in the New Testament, in which Jesus is often shown appealing to the things of nature in order to illustrate the way in which God deals with his creatures.

But on the other hand we must be clear about the limitations to which I have just referred. We cannot get to know God's real nature without his help, unless he reveals himself to us, shows us what he is. And we have to realize that although as believers we can see the hand of God in the things of the world, others who do not share our belief cannot. In other words we see because we believe: we do not believe because we see. An opponent might therefore say that Christians are merely imposing upon the world a meaning and a significance which is not there. If it were there, they might add, then anyone could see it and they would be as much aware of it as we are.

But this is a fallacious argument, though it has some truth in it. When we look at the world as Christians, we do indeed see significance in a greater degree than others, for we have found the key to its meaning. But that does not mean that there is nothing for the others to find. On the contrary the world and men's experiences within it raise questions, to which no answer can be given except that which Christ gives.

The objection that, if this significance were there, others would be able to see it by simple observation is shown to be false in many fields of life. We could think of many forms of personal relationship which can only have meaning to those who are engaged in them—family love for example. The full meaning of love within a family can only be known by those who are participating in it. Certain things can be observed from outside, but the meaning can be missed, although these outside observations can only be fully explained by the light which is thrown on them by the love.

It is surely at this point, the point of love, even in its imperfect human expressions, that a merely intellectual approach to the problems of the world is seen to be inadequate in regard to human life, and consequently much more inadequate in relation to God. It is our experience of love which should lead us to God, for this experience touches depths of human life which are quite outside the merely 'natural' in a scientific sense. This is one of the things which I find most puzzling about those who say that they must move solely within the realm of scientific enquiry and experiment, and maintain that outside that field we cannot

45

find anything of certain value. God, they say, is not to be known in any form which is recognizable as knowledge by the modern scientific man. The puzzling element to me is that this approach rules out everything which makes ordinary human life most worth while. It excludes human love at a level higher than can be explained merely on physical and mental levels; it excludes any real content in our deepest aesthetic experiences of painting or music or poetry. In short the approach seems to make nonsense of what the best men think to be the most important part of human life.

Our life is full of deep and mysterious currents and experiences which fill the outer life with a rich inner content. When we say that the things which we know in the world can point to God, we include all these wonderful experiences which enlighten our everyday life. We admit that they cannot of themselves tell us what God is like, unless God himself reveals the truth to us, but even these things are the reflections (however distorted or muddled) through his work of the God who has made all that is. They can bring us part of the way, and, when we have the fuller understanding of God, they are seen to have very great significance and meaning.

What brings us from one stage to the next from enquiry to sight? The answer is faith. But we have to understand what is meant by 'faith' in the full Christian sense. It is not a blind acceptance of things which ordinary people find incredible. Basically, it is an act of commitment, which we undertake by a free choice of our own. This freedom is an essential element in faith. One sometimes hears people say that they wish they had so-and-so's faith, as though that faith were a sort of prize won in the draw for premium bonds. But, basically, faith is a decision, a choice on the part of the person concerned to commit himself in trust to God. 'How can I get faith?' a man once asked. He received the reply: 'From now on decide to do everything and make all your choices as if you had faith, and you will find it.' 'Faith', said Dean Inge, 'begins with an experiment and ends with an experience.' Faith is first of all a choice, which any man can make, and when he makes it, God is there to make the gift sure.

This faith is an act of trust, that is to say, it is allied to love, and this is where the true Christian understanding is so vital. Christianity will not allow faith in its full sense to be merely a calculation of the mind, of what is the best chance: it insists that it be an act of trusting commitment, which means a commitment to a God of love in Christ. And here a parallel with our normal experiences of love is illuminating.

Though care must be taken not to press analogies too far, the act of faith surely has parallels in human life: it is not something entirely separate, which applies only to our relationship with God. The nearest similarity seems to me to be in marriage, the root of which is the commitment of the parties to one another in faith. Faith is always concerned with the partly unknown, even in human life, and love partakes of this character. Love must have risk within it to make it true love. A love which depends on some kind of demonstrable proof is not love at all, but a mathematical equation. Love must be commitment to the partly unknown, for this is the essential element in growing personal relations between people. A reflec-

47

tion of the truth of our relationship to God can be seen here.

Faith, then, is not something for which we have to wait passively, either in hope or despair: it is rather a step which God is waiting for men to take, but which he will not force upon them either physically, mentally, or spiritually. But, when it is taken, everything falls into place, and we see that nothing else could explain the universe. We take the step of faith and find in amazement that it has made the world take meaning, coherence, and purpose.

We have already touched upon the importance of seeing the universe as a moving dynamic cosmos, and not as a static immovable fixture. In the past, when this static idea was paramount, Christ was certainly loved and known by those who tried to follow him. But it was more difficult to make the fact of Christ fit in fully with such a universe. He appeared, if one can say so, as a sort of visitor, who came for a time and then went off to be in heaven. Of course he is known to be living, but this did not bring him into the world's movement, as he appears in it when we see this dynamic movement in its full force. Teilhard wished to emphasize that to understand truly the place of Christ was to see him as giving meaning to the whole process, and also at the same time to be the embodiment of what the world is becoming and will one day be. He coined another word 'Christification' for this presents a future process of the world. What can it mean to say that the world will be made Christ, 'christified'? With some diffidence, I would suggest that its basic meaning is this: just as Christ is the total embodiment of God in the world, that is to say, in Christ we find man, and hence the universe, as it is intended to be, totally united to

God in love and obedience, so this is the end which is destined for the whole cosmos, when it will be with Christ totally united to God in love and unity.

This is the fulfilment of the passages in the New Testament, which are so strong, about the end of the world. They are pictures of the future in forms which we do not always find congenial in our own day. Nevertheless they point to the gathering up into one of all the scattered elements of the universe, according to the plan of God which is running through them all, but which depends on the response of man for its final fulfilment. In other days this was thought of in terms of human judgements and natural portents. But our further insights enable us to see it as a much closer integration of man and the universe into God. If this is a true way of looking at the universe, it needs changes in our own outlook. It does not mean that we have to throw overboard any of the truths which we already know in our experience as Christians, but it may mean, and for most of us it will mean, vastly expanding the horizons of our minds, when we consider the action of Christ in the world. We are prone to see Christ far too much in merely religious terms, and this shortcoming of many Christians is one of the attitudes against which protests are being made, both inside and outside Christian circles. It is a prime heresy of the most dangerous kind to think that God is only interested in religion. If we put it as crudely as that, there will be few of us who would plead guilty to the charge of holding that view, but, if we rigidly examine our own underlying attitudes, we shall find that we are always falling into the trap of assuming that religion is the main sphere of God's influence.

Yet we are always telling one another that 'God so

loved the *world*':—that ought to be a sufficient safe-guard against these dangers. But it isn't, because when we see that God is active in his Church in a special and particular way, we assume without further thought that that is where we can confine our attention. If it is true that those outside the Christian church ought to look for God's action within it, then it is equally true that those inside must learn to see Christ's working in men who have nothing to do with the Christian churches so far as we can see, and also see him in the universe in all its variety and richness.

Teilhard de Chardin points us to the grandeur of the development of the cosmos as witnessing the work of Christ in the universe.

How does this give meaning to the universe? How does it explain its purpose? When we look at the cosmos in these terms, we see God greater than and beyond the universe, yet sustaining it, directing it, binding it together, himself in it through his actions. For God is to be found in a real sense wherever he is acting. He is to be seen within the world drawing it into a unity with himself through the high point of the world—man—now conscious of his spiritual poten-tialities, aware of his knowledge and power, though not yet completely developed. Man it is who is to guide and form the evolving cosmos through his own efforts, both scientific and religious, until the consummation comes in perfect unity with the God who made it and is redeeming it.

So as to bring the inner truth of this great work home to man God had to act, and did act, in such a manner as would demonstrate to men the reality of his own penetration of the world and reveal to them the depth of his own union with our human nature. This

revelation is Christ, through whom God himself is identified with the human race, not in any self-enclosed way,
but in a way which illuminates the meaning of the
world and brings into it new life. 'That was the true
light which lightens every man coming into the world':
this surely is the same thought. These insights are the
authentic echo of the teaching of St John's Gospel
where again we see the coming of Christ in a cosmic
setting. 'The Word was God. All things were made by
him . . .In him was life and the life was the light of
men . . . as many as received him to them gave he power
to become sons of God. And the Word was made flesh
and dwelt among us.' We are back to the very truths
which St John was setting out, and which can have a
new inspiration for the men of our time.

'The incarnation', said Teilhard (*Hymn of the
Universe*, p. 144), 'means the renewal, the restoration,
of all the energies and powers of the universe; Christ
is the instrument, the Centre and End of all creation,
animate *and* material; through him everything is
created, hallowed, quickened. This is the constant,
*general* teaching of St John and St Paul (that most
'cosmic' of sacred writers), a teaching which has passed
into the most solemn phrases of the liturgy, but which
we repeat and which future generations will go on
repeating to the end without ever being able to master
or to measure its profound and mysterious meaning,
bound up as it is with the comprehension of the
universe.'

All this, it may be said, is mystical insight rather
than detached reason. But we must realize that there
is no clash between the two, and indeed that one is
needed in order to supplement the other. Nor is it
claimed that this aspect of the significance of Christ in

51

any way exhausts what Christ must mean to man. Indeed, as we know, there is no end to the content of what Christ can mean to those who know him and his action in the world. Our minds are limited in what they can grasp at one time, and we easily fall into the habit of concentrating on one thing at a time—perhaps we have to do this. And from that position it is easy to adopt a bad habit of only looking at certain aspects of Christ which happen to appeal to us, or which are easier for us to understand and leaving out the rest. To concentrate on only one part of the significance of Christ may call in question the other parts which are equally needed for a balanced viewpoint.

And so we find in these ideas that evolution, matter, movement, incompleteness, are illuminated by the figure of Christ who fulfils in himself the whole meaning of the universe and its relation to God. To see Christ in this way changes our attitudes to many things, including science and knowledge. Instead of thinking in terms of a clash between science and religion, as many still do, we suddenly perceive that this is the very opposite of the truth, and that science on the contrary is in itself an essentially religious activity, in the proper sense of the word. When St Paul wrote that God was in Christ reconciling the world to himself (2 Corinthians 5:9) it is constricting to confine the statement merely to some personal relation which we may have with God, though of course this is included. St Paul's sentence concerns the very nature of the cosmos and its potentialities in the light of Christ's appearance.

There remain unsolved problems which we have not even mentioned, for example the problem of evil. How does evil originate and how is it related to a God of love, who is redeeming the world? There is no full intellectual explanation of the mystery of evil and suffering. Their presence in the world, and the ways in which they are known, cannot be met with a simple reply which will easily satisfy those who have seen and known their reality. But the message of Christ announces that both evil and suffering can be made to serve the highest cause of love, when they are brought within the ambit of God's action. It is not for nothing that we have as the symbol of our religion a cross from which was heard the cry of dereliction and suffering. Christianity does not claim to 'explain' suffering, but it has entered into it and found through it the path to victory and triumph.

Here Christ is the key, not primarily for the intellect but for life. For he did not come to explain but to live suffering, not to indite evil but to undergo its full consequences. 'It is in the Passion of Christ that the ultimate secret of man's destiny is at once unveiled and unfolded. Only the invisible Lamb can break the seals that have kept the book of fate closed. He unveils it by revealing the depth of misery, the true nature of sin, the power of the forces of evil. It is in the light of the Cross that man knows what he is' (Daniélou, *Christ and Us*, p. 139).

Teilhard de Chardin's outlook was suffused with a living faith in God, from which sprang his convictions about the nature of the universe. Evil to him seemed the reverse side of the developing good, inevitable in the process of advance in which there have to be accidents and failures. The liberating process which he acclaims is accompanied 'by suffering, set-backs and even apparent disasters' (*Future of Man*, p. 231, n.), but this is more understandable in a universe in evolution than it is in one thought of as static. When we do give ourselves to hear and accept the Word of God, however it may come to us, then the problem of evil is not abolished, but is defeated by the creative and positive forces of the love of God. That love of God is known in one way alone, and that way is Christ—the key to the meaning of the universe.

# [3]

## *Where is the world going?*

IF SOMEONE asks where we are going, we may as a counter-question ask whether we are going anywhere, or indeed whether we are going at all. Movement in the universe we have seen to be the basis of the insights of some thinkers, but perhaps those who take this view are still in a minority. There is certainly a very large section of Christian opinion which still thinks in wholly static terms, which does not see the importance of understanding movement as part of the nature of the cosmos. The contrast between the two groups has been well drawn by Teilhard de Chardin at the beginning of an essay about progress (*Future of Man,* p. 11).

'It is a pleasant and dramatic spectacle, that of Mankind divided to its very depths into two irrevocably opposed camps—one looking towards the horizon and proclaiming with all its new-found faith, "We are moving", and the other, without shifting its position, obstinately maintaining, "Nothing changes. We are not moving at all".

'These latter, the "immobilists", though they lack

passion (immobility has never inspired anyone with enthusiasm!), have common sense on their side, habit of thought, inertia, pessimism and also, to some extent, morality and religion. Nothing, they argue, appears to have changed since man began to hand down the memory of the past, not the undulations of the earth, or the forms of life, or the genius of Man or even his goodness. Thus far practical experimentation has failed to modify the fundamental characteristics of even the most humble plant. Human suffering, vice and war, although they may momentarily abate recur from age to age with an increasing virulence. Even the striving after progress contributes to the sum of evil: to effect change is to undermine the painfully established traditional order whereby the distress of living creatures was reduced to a minimum. What innovator has not re-tapped the springs of blood and tears? For the sake of human tranquility, in the name of Fact, and in defence of the sacred Established Order, the immobilists forbid the earth to move. Nothing changes, they say, or can change. The raft must drift purposelessly on a shoreless sea.

'But the other half of mankind, startled by the lookout's cry, has left the huddle where the rest of the crew sit with their heads together telling time-honoured tales. Gazing out over the dark sea they study for themselves the lapping of waters along the hull of the craft that bears them, breathe the scents borne to them on the breeze, gaze at the shadows cast from pole to pole by a changeless eternity. And for all these things, while remaining separately the same—the ripple of water, the scent of the air, the lights in the sky—become linked together and acquire a new sense: the fixed and random Universe is seen to move.

'No one who has seen this vision can be restrained from guarding and proclaiming it.'

There is a romantic quality about this presentation which may perhaps conceal the reality of the differences which it describes. For there can be no doubt that the concept of movement in the world does make an immense difference in a man's outlook, not only in worldly things but in the things of God. For the nature of God himself is to be seen through the way he works, and a God who is engaged closely in a moving and developing world is a different kind of God from one who is detached from it and acts mainly on it from his position of detachment. There can be no doubt that it is the active, near-at-hand God concerned with the world who is the God of the Christian faith.

If we are to penetrate more deeply into the meaning of this cosmic movement, we must turn our attention to the part which mankind is destined to play in the whole operation. The idea of progress which was popular in the last century and the beginning of this has been largely discredited. Hardly anyone believes in it any more. It was a concept of progress for mankind as he secured more and more control over science and gradually mastered the world, so as to govern it to the benefit of man and to exclude from it all those disagreeable features which marred life for him. There seemed to be no limit to the riches and success which industry and the advance of technology could bring. But although this attitude is no longer held in these rather crude terms by thinking people, aspects of it are constantly cropping up in some form or other. Some writers appeal basically to the same kind of human self-satisfaction as the original idea of progress in the nineteenth century. By closely linking technopolis with the kingdom of God, they give to a passing social state which is the outcome of technical achievement a semi-religious glow, tending to make it good in itself.

There are too many contradictory facts for the idea of inevitable human progress to be easily defended. Two world wars in this century, together with the incredible deliberate torture and slaughter of millions of innocent human beings, have been the marks of a civilization which grew out of the society which encouraged belief in human progress. The condition of the world today does not give much ground for supposing that the fundamental problems of human relations are yet being solved with success. Conflicts between and within nations are the common stock of our daily news.

But in spite of all these horrors, the thought of progress itself in its cosmic sense need not be rejected merely because a more partial and inadequate view has to be abandoned. If we put progress into the dimension of the universe, the cosmic dimension, and regard it as meaning that the plan of God for the world continues to its inevitable climax within the framework of his purpose, then the idea of progress is re-established, both as something credible, and also as inescapable, if we believe in a God on whom all else depends. For his purpose cannot be completely defeated, even within the free circle of man's choice, since all the activity of the cosmos, whether human or not, takes place within the total providence of God himself. Movement towards the end which he has appointed can rightly be called progress. The presentation of the truth of evolution in what Teilhard calls *cosmogenesis* is a form of discernible progress which seems to shadow a creative purpose, gradually being fulfilled and yet to come to its completion: movement towards this completion is progress.

'The truth can now be seen', he writes (*Future of Man*, p. 19). 'Progress is not what the popular mind looks for, finding with exasperation that it never comes. Progress is not immediate ease, well-being and peace. It is not rest. It is not even, directly, virtue. Essentially progress is a *force*, and the most dangerous of forces. It is the Consciousness of all that is and all that can be. Though it may encounter every kind of prejudice and resentment, this must be asserted because it is the truth: to *be* more is in the first place to *know* more.'

These few sentences introduce the part of our subject to which we must now give more attention, namely the question as to what part man is to play in all this. Where does he fit in? It is all very well to speak of these vast forces of developing evolution, but, if all that is true, does it not make man a pawn of forces beyond himself, so that he is found to be little more than a puppet in the play of irresistible forces outside his control?

The answer to such questions as this depends on the view we take as to the connexion between the universe as a whole and the place of man in it. If we look at the cosmos as essentially separate from man, and see mankind as something added to the rest as a sort of extra, then it would be difficult to fit him in to this evolutionary concept of present and future. This has certainly been the way in which many Christians have been accustomed to regard the situation. But it is just this habit which needs to be queried. And we must note that we are not asked merely to give up one theory and substitute another for it: the matter goes much deeper.

We have to go behind the theories and question the unconsidered presuppositions which lie behind them, a more difficult and radical process.

It is necessary to see the world in a different light, in a way to which we have already given attention. Our view of man is vitally affected by this new light, for he is seen not only to be an integral part of the material universe, but to have evolved out of it, so that, in a sort of way, all his potentialities were present in the undeveloped world out of which he has himself evolved and is still evolving. But whereas in the past the unconscious world has been developing by what we may call 'chance', though within the overall plan of creation, now the consciousness and freedom of man has put into his hands the power to shape its future.

Matter and spirit, we have seen, are not different *things* but are aspects of the universe. The growth of self-consciousness in man gives him the opportunity to make the universe into what it is meant to be, a spiritualized material world growing towards its consummation in unity with its Creator, its climax in God.

It is self-consciousness which makes men different from all other forms of life in the world. Animals know things, as we can see from simple observation and from the fact that we can teach our domestic animals all sorts of tricks, if we have patience enough. Animals themselves learn and acquire knowledge in some sense. But man alone knows that he knows: only he has the self-conscious knowledge which is another name, and perhaps a better one, for what has usually been called reason, the power of reflection.

Man therefore finds himself at the directing point of the universe, and the immense increase in scientific knowledge in recent years should have brought home to him the immensity of his power and hence the immensity of his choices. It is an interesting fact that at the same time as we find a tendency to hold that men are not free in what they do, how they think, and how things develop, there is a parallel experience which denies this. For we know that our powers of destruction have increased so vastly that it is now perfectly possible, one might even say fairly easy, for man to destroy all human life on this planet. In other words we are faced with developments in science which make our choice clearer rather than dimmer. Man faces the choice, both of acquiring more knowledge, and, when he has acquired it, of using it either in a constructive or a destructive way. And no theories can take away the stark fact that a choice of vast magnitude is set before us, just as it is in lesser matters when we have to live our life day by day.

The significance of this in the framework of the evolutionary idea is that, instead of mere 'chance', the evolution of the universe is directed by the choices which man now has it in his power to make. As more and more he increases his knowledge of the workings of the universe, so he is able to make definite choices as to how he wishes it to develop, and at the same time he is affecting his own development by increasing his capacities for knowledge, and therefore of choice. Thus we can see that in this way he is acquiring all the time a greater moral responsibility for the future of man and of the universe, for he is more and more the decisive element in deciding the direction in which it shall evolve.

If we look back at the past and see how the world developed, and evolved, we see that it came out of innumerable small apparently haphazard elements, which by a combination of factors produced various lines of development. This is to be found in the history of living things. Some of these lines continued and flourished; others gradually disappeared. It is not possible to discern any special reason why one branch should have gone and one should have continued. Parallel to this historical development the freedom and responsibility of man also includes innumerable small elements in the whole, but now his deliberate choices have a contribution to play in forming the direction of the whole, so that man's influence is not limited to decisions on a world scale, making them on behalf of the whole of mankind, though this would be one important form of such choices. The way in which mankind and the world will develop depends on all the tiny choices made all over the world all the time by individual men. They could make the wrong choices, choices which lead to extinction and not to growth, and it is this which makes the freedom of man.

This conception of man's freedom in no way denies the traditional way of looking at his responsibility: on the contrary it establishes it and extends its importance, since it links the effect of exercising freedom of choice with the development of the whole universe and thus gives his choice cosmic dimensions. Moral despair and cynicism is often bound up with the feeling that the great course of events in the world is unaffected by what the individual does. But when we put the matter in this wider setting we envisage an unbreakable connection between the act of the individual person and the whole state of the world and the process in which it is involved.

This again links up with the Christian understanding of the work of Christ. For his entry into the world is seen to be, not merely a concern with man as a separate form of life on the surface of the earth, but with the bringing to fruition, the redeeming of the whole cosmos. Man is a key element in this, and God's incarnation in Christ is the means by which God reaches down to us, identifies himself with our life and the life of the world, and brings it forward on the road which leads to its final end in God through Christ. The imperfections and failures of the world, both in man and outside him, are brought again into relation with God, and become the means by which the world comes nearer to God when they are brought into relation with the act of unity in Christ which God has done. Then the things which are out of true are brought back to him who is the truth.

We may then go on to ask what are the means by which the rôle of man is made more effective in the whole process of a cosmos evolving in accordance with the intention of God. And here the importance of education has been especially stressed by Teilhard in an approach which has some fascinating possibilities. It is of course generally recognized that through heredity certain characteristics are passed on from one generation of animals to the next. There is a growing adaptability of certain types, which become more and more adapted to their surroundings and environment so as to exhibit a developing ability to meet the needs of life. This would appear to indicate that, however slowly, there is learning which is passed on by heredity. We normally think of education as an activity only in terms of human beings, but is this really so? Surely in the experiences of the animal world we see a sort of biological education which is passed on from one generation to another, so that acquired characteristics

63

are passed on to others. Teilhard writes: 'We have only to observe the animal world with minds more open to the ideas of birth and evolution to perceive, in this as in every case, that the "human" could not exist if it did not contain, transfigured in terms of mind, a property common to all animals, of which the beginnings are to be detected as they vanish into the past. The dog, the cat or the bird train their young in countless ways to hunt, to fly or to build a nest. The monkey does much more. And how are we to explain the remarkable behaviour-patterns of the beaver, or of insects, except as the outcome of accumulated and transmitted experiences and discoveries? Such phenomena become apparent to us only where the creature under study has attained a sufficient degree of spontaneity, still more if it lives in a group. But what more is needed to persuade us that, at least for practical purposes, education is a universal biological function, co-existent with the totality of the living world?' (*Future of Man*, pp. 27-8).

Human education then may be seen, not merely as something which individuals acquire for the purpose of making their own way in the world, or even of contributing to the good of the general community, but as something which is added to mankind and remains with him, being incorporated into succeeding generations as an additional ability or capacity. It is an additive in the biological sense.

This idea seems once more to emphasize the responsibility of the freedom of man. By the way in which we are educating ourselves we are in fact forming future generations who will come after us, not by example but by actually affecting the kind of people our successors will be, and, as we become conscious of this fact, we begin to see how great is our responsibility for the whole future of the world.

All this links up with another conviction (already mentioned), namely that for man knowledge is being, to know more is to partake more fully in the essential being of the universe. Here is an important possible bridge between science and religion: it is not a matter of arguing for or against some particular interpretation of historical events, but an insight into the quality, the essential character of the underlying life of both science and religion. Without wishing to play on words in any superficial way, one can at once notice a close correspondence even in the language of science and religion. If we read the Gospel of St John, we shall find that knowledge is another word for life and light: in science the pursuit of knowledge is the whole purpose of its activities. It is true that at first glance the word 'knowledge' seems to be used of two different things, but is this really the case? In both the basic concept of knowledge is surely an insight into the nature of things, that is, into the reality which underlies the facts and incidents which we observe and can identify and record. And at this point any kind of knowledge which is true is indeed the source of a more intensive life. To know more is to be more.

Knowledge also brings power, and with power comes responsibility. Responsibility may and probably will extend rapidly in areas in which at present we are only on the fringe. New techniques in eugenics and breeding which have been applied to animals on a wide scale are becoming available for human beings, and, however much we may revolt against applying animal standards to men and women, the fact that we have the power to do so gives us a positive responsibility to think

c

out what this means, certainly not merely in animal terms, but equally certainly it must be thought out in human terms. It needs no scientific training to read suggestions that chemists are on the verge of discoveries which may make it possible to produce life. We should not quail at the prospect even though it may mean the radical rethinking of the way in which we have hitherto spoken and thought, for we can put no limits on God by forbidding him to give us the power of reproducing life itself. We already have it in one form—that of sexual reproduction: would it be at variance with what we know of God to find that he has given power to make life by other means also?

We see then a vision of dynamic development in which man is playing and is to play a guiding and decisive part. In the process of doing so he is changing himself into a fuller and richer being, in particular through increasing knowledge and the process of education in which he is involved. 'Materialism' is the wrong understanding of all this process, for it makes the outward shell the measure of everything else. But there is an essential sense in which the material is a vital part of the spiritual, both material and spiritual being two aspects of everything that exists as part of the cosmos.

Although Christians are frequently to be heard accusing other people of being materialists, it is often they themselves who are the materialists. This is an example of the common fault of attacking in other people those characteristics which are really one's own faults, though the person who has them is often blind to them. A materialist is one who refuses to see or allow a spiritual aspect or content in matter. And Christians have often in the past, and still frequently do, divide the world mentally into the material and the spiritual. When they do so they are in effect saying that there *is* a part of the world where there is matter without spirit, to which spirit cannot be properly attached. To do this is materialism in the rankest sense, as it banishes the spiritual from part of God's creation.

This is a difficult point for us to grasp, because it is a rejection of the way in which we usually think, and it is difficult indeed to use our thinking process to condemn the habits into which that very thinking process has fallen. We often think of the religious man as the spiritual man, that is, the spiritual man is he who is interested in the things of God, by which we mean prayer and religious services and preaching and reading the Bible and so on. The material man is he who confines his interests to material things like money, or science.

But it is right to think of the spiritual man as he who interests himself in the things of God. The things of God are the whole created universe and everything in it, therefore the scientist is just as spiritual as the man who studies the Bible, if he is pursuing his investigations into the things of God in the true spirit of scientific enquiry, for that is the means which God has given man for the purpose of acquiring knowledge. And acquiring knowledge of the truth, whether it is religious truth, or scientific truth, or engineering truth is, in the proper sense of the word, a 'spiritual' activity, whether it is accompanied by the singing of hymns or not—to put it crudely.

Money is somewhat different in that a man may confine his interest to money and make the acquisition of money his sole aim in life. In this case of course he is not indulging in a spiritual occupation. Nevertheless

67

do not let us overlook the fact that the economic processes by which the modern world alone can live are themselves spiritual processes in so far as they are pursued for the right reason. When Christians try to restrict the quality of the spiritual to specific 'religious' activities, they are really showing themselves to be crude materialists by robbing these other sides of human activity of their true spiritual dimension.

Having said all this, we must ask the vital question as to where it is all leading. Is there a future to which we may reasonably look forward? And, if so, what is the place of man and of the Church in it?

Teilhard sees two possibilities before the world in its future evolution. One of them goes in the direction of dispersal and individualist divergence, so that the world becomes more and more broken up into different elements. The separate distinct individual is seen as the most important manifestation of life and being.

The other looks forward to a convergence, a coming together more and more of all the various elements in the world, brought together in this process under the leadership of man. But, because man has consciousness and the power to choose, the future can no longer be for him a matter of chance or of blind instinct, as it has been for lower forms of life or pre-life. He must make a choice and decide what he is to pursue, and here he must take stock of what he knows to be the highest form of his own nature.

This choice is a form of the alternatives before every man constantly throughout his life. The choice is one fraught with big consequences, yet it is shown in small, frequent, every day, decisions: it is the choice between self-centredness and unselfishness, or between making the individual the be-all and end-all of life, and choosing on the other hand to make personal relations, that is service to others, the end of effort and purpose. The former leads to the break up of society into small warring units: the latter to community and personal fulfilment within it.

For the Christian there can be no doubt as to which he must choose, for his whole faith comes to a practical head at this point. But apart from this, it is common observation that personal fulfilment comes through personal relations with others and in no other way. This is another aspect of the spiritual and basic truth expressed by Jesus Himself in telling us that it is the man who seeks his own life who will lose it, and the man who loses it for the sake of others who will find fulfilment.

In the insights which we have been trying to share we see how this personal choice is identical with the future of the whole universe. In making his personal choices man is in fact deciding which way the whole cosmos will develop. Observation tells us that it is moving towards a greater unity, and that man has to find out what this means for him and the world. It is perhaps because we are standing at a decisive point in the development of the universe that we meet in such strength the warring forces which hold back or try to reverse the process of fulfilment. It is commonplace nowadays to say that we live in a shrinking world. We see by looking round us how the immense speed of scientific discovery and application has brought people together in a way never before known. Of course we are not adjusted to it: this adjustment takes time and for many it is a painful experience. But unless it takes place and is seen in its right importance, there will be worse experiences to face. We are being forced into unity with one another, whether we like it or not, and, if we ask what are the forces which are having this effect, we must answer that they are the growing discovery of truth through science. In other words the truth which has been preached by the Christian religion and which has become less and less effective in recent years is being replaced by the same truth forced upon us by other means. Is this the hand of God, who insists that we learn the truth by some means or other? Is it a reflection of the failure of Christians to see the hand of God outside their own borders or the borders of their organized Churches? Whether this be so or not, it is plain enough that it is a Christian obligation to broaden the understanding of this truth whatever its source.

The unity of mankind may develop in ways we have not yet envisaged. It may bring men together in a closer relationship in which the individual elements on which we at present set value have much less place. Does this mean that personal values will become less important or disappear altogether? On the contrary: it means the opposite. We have to realize that true union en-hances personal values: it does not diminish them. We know this to be the case in married life, for example: even more we know it to be the case in our relations with God. It is the closest possible union with God which is the aim of the Christian life, as we learn from the reported words of Jesus himself in St John's Gospel. 'As thou Father art in me and I in thee, that they may be in us'. What more powerful statement than that could be made?

Personal fulfilment is to be found here alone. Unity is the inevitable outcome of love when it is true, a love which is made by the Spirit of God. This is and always has been the heart of the Christian message. It is the Gospel of the love of God that it goes to all lengths to bring about the unity with the world which has been broken or which has not been achieved. 'Love has always been carefully eliminated from realist and positivist concepts of the world; but sooner or later we shall have to acknowledge that it is the fundamental impulse of Life, or, if you prefer, the one natural medium in which the rising course of evolution can proceed. With love omitted there is truly nothing ahead of us except the forbidding prospect of standardization and enslavement—the doom of ants and termites. It is through love and within love that we must look for the deepening of our deepest self, in the life-giving coming together of humankind' (*Future of Man*, pp. 54-5).

There are then dangers in the drawing together of mankind, dangers which arise through socialization without soul, union without love. This is why it is so vital that the vision of what the universe really is should be extended even to those who do not follow the normal paths of Christian practice and belief. The Christian faith has something to say to them about their own activities and responsibilities in their own fields, which can perhaps inspire them with a vision which also sees the essential truth which all men must accept or perish.

Christ is the key again here. He it is who gives meaning to the movement of the world and reveals the secret plan of God and the means by which it can be achieved. It is he who gives us the assurance of an active God outside the universe who nevertheless is identified with it by his own action. But he does not only give us a key to the meaning of the past and the present: he also shows us the future, for Christ him-

71

self is the embodiment of what the whole cosmos is to be. He came to initiate a new stage in the process of bringing the world to God and leading it forward through his own life to the only life which could bring it to the end prepared for it by God. Here we see how Christ is directly related to the end of the world. It throws a new and helpful light on that part of the New Testament which is concerned with the last things. We know very well that the first Christians were intensely taken up with the coming last things, and scholars are constantly repeating how important the last things and the end of the world were in the teaching of Jesus and in the minds of his followers. And although the early Christians foreshortened the end and saw things in a telescoped sort of way which did not allow for the stretch of years which lay between, yet they were completely right in the truth which they perceived. For Christ's appearance is the beginning of the end which has not yet occurred and towards which he and we are working.

Consider this passage from St Paul, well known to all Christians: 'As in Adam all men die, so in Christ all will be brought to life; but each in his own proper place: Christ the first fruits, and afterwards, at his coming, those who belong to Christ. Then comes the end, when he delivers up the kingdom to God the Father, after abolishing every kind of domination, authority, and power. For he is destined to reign until God has put all enemies under his feet; and the last enemy to be abolished is death. Scripture says, "He has put all things in subjection under his feet". But in saying "all things", it clearly means to exclude God who subordinates them; and when all things are thus subject to him, then the Son himself will also be made subordinate to God who made all things subject to him' (1 Corinthians 15:22-8, *NEB*).

Here we see St Paul's vision of the end when Christ delivers up all things to the Father, that is to say, the end of all things will be their unity in Christ, so that Christ is not only, as we have been accustomed to think of him, the historical Christ of revelation, but he is also the end and fulfilment of evolution in the creative and redemptive plan of God.

A tribute to Teilhard was written by a Protestant Pastor in the following words: 'It seems to me that the great originality on the religious plane of Teilhard de Chardin . . . is to have brought Christianity back to the vision of the universal Christ, of the cosmic Christ. This spiritual advance is contained in an extension of the highest flights of Johannine and Pauline thought. At such a level the doctrine of the Redemption finally takes on its true religious dimension; it is no longer expressed in juridical terms, which are far too human and limited, but in a love that embraces the totality of men and the totality of worlds. It is that love, a love on the scale of God, that illuminates with its clarity, at once magnificent and comforting, a truly eschatological vision of the meaning of being and of life' (*Cuénot*, p. 393).

So Christ is the beginning, the centre, and the end. The insights of Christians have kept glowing the truths which are needed to lighten every other part of the world's work and development. But Christians must not be ownerconscious about Christ: they must not think that he is their Christ and no one else's. For they ought to be proclaiming that he is the world's Christ. Too often we hug him to ourselves and tell others that they cannot have any of him unless they adopt our views and our interpretations and put aside those of others. This is a form of betrayal of Christ of which Christians are particularly guilty. Part of the hope for the world must depend on the expansion of the vision of Christians who though they rightly know that they have a knowledge of the truth, do not see how they often restrict this knowledge and hem it in through their limited sight.

And at this point we must enquire where the Church is to play a role in the new situation. The Church has and does play a vital part in passing on to new generations the grasp of the truth which it has inherited, an aspect of the truth which could have been secured in no other fashion than this. We do not underestimate the gifts which we have been given through the Church, but it has been guilty of narrowness. Would we not already be united in our Christian witness, if it were not for the pettiness and narrownesses which we have permitted to be associated with our real understandings of the truth? And not only that, we have been over-possessive of the truth, as though it would die if it were not kept warm and cosy within our ecclesiastical structures. But the truth only lives and flourishes in the fresh air, to which we must continually expose it.

The truth which we have seen must be passed on to those outside the Church, and we must learn what truths are to be found there, outside our systems of thought and Christian practice. We have often wanted to capture the truth, and keep it within the Churches and to say in effect that it is all there. Now it is perfectly true that there are important sides of life which can only be found by living the life of Christ within the Christian community. But, if we look for the Christian community, we eventually have to choose one of the actual forms of the Church which we meet on earth, although none of these is the Christian community as it ought to be. One obvious reason is that the Christian community cannot be fully grown until Christian divisons are done away, and the Christian community cannot be found in its fulness until all men are part of it.

Alongside this true life of the Church and of its members, there is truth outside. And do not let us forget that the Church itself is a community for the whole world. As Christ is himself the centre and fulfilment of the universe, so also the Church is to be Christ among men, where alone mankind is fulfilled. It has therefore a reference to men outside as well as to men within it. This is a mystery: nevertheless it should lead us to put aside all those exclusive and narrow concepts of the Church of Christ which made the Church so much smaller than the Church's Lord, who is its head.

There are therefore two main objectives of the Church in the promoting of the life of Christ in the world. And it must never be forgotten that the Church only acquires meaning in its relation to Christ. It is itself the product of Christ's life, death, and rising to life again through the Spirit. It is sometimes called the extension of the Incarnation, but this is too static a phrase and has become encrusted with fixed ideas. It would be better to say that the Church is the instrument of Christ, Christ himself in whom God is alive and active in the world, bringing men to better knowledge of God through his Spirit.

The Church has the task of bringing more and more men to know Christ deeply within its fellowship. It must recognize, as we have said, the truth which men outside it have to bring into it, and, at the same time,

75

complete that knowledge with the knowledge which comes only through that life of unity which the Gospel of love must create. In doing this the Church is living beforehand the last things which all must come to know. In this sense the Church too is an eschatological community, a fellowship which is living the last things now. Unhappily it does this very imperfectly, but in trying to be Christ, the Church with Christ its head partakes in the life and work of Christ. In him and in it should be found the perfecting of that unity, that love, to which the whole cosmos is tending.

In the second place the Church brings to all men whether inside or outside her borders, an increasing awareness of the meaning of Christ present and active in all his different ways in the world. To do this Christians have to wake out of their contented sleep and broaden their minds to meet the sort of challenges which we have been examining.

Teilhard himself was convinced that the Church was essential for the fully human to develop, as he believed that only the Church was capable of stimulating human energy thoroughly and in its entirety (*Cuénot*, p. 367). When we look at this task in its widest perspective our own divisions appear as they are, petty and relatively minor. We see, moreover, in a clearer light, what no doubt we have already perceived, that the Church cannot possibly fulfil its function if it denies in its actions what it proclaims in its words. Love must mean unity: the two are really words for the same thing. A Gospel of love which seems to consider unity of secondary importance will not convince anyone of anything, and will at the same time be at odds with the whole trend of the world's development.

But this unity needs to be seen in the right perspective of the whole of God's plan for the world. It is so easy to make our aim a little unity, which in a way may even impoverish and weaken the idea of unity itself by being content with something which is not worthy of the name, and which has no discernible connection with love. Let me repeat: when we use the word 'unity' as Christians we are using it as another word for love made to come to action, and when we use the word 'love' we mean a love which cannot be expressed except in unity. This is why for our own sake and the sake of the Church, as well as for those outside it, our vision must be stretched to see God's plan in a wider perspective than that we are used to. Then Christian unity becomes even more urgent and more meaningful.

We have now found the answer to our question where is the world going—the world is going to Christ. In this process which is the work of the Spirit of God the life of the Church has an indispensable part to play, and within it the lives and the choices of its members, the Christians of today and the coming years. We see that Christ is in the world as well as in the Church, and that it is by this vision of Christ and our own unity with him and his work that the world is being brought to God and to his fulfilment.

Perhaps these words of Teilhard de Chardin may sum up what we have been thinking of: 'Since Jesus was born, and grew to his full stature, and died, everything has continued to move forward *because Christ is not yet fully formed*: he has not yet gathered about him the last folds of his robe of flesh and love which is made up of his faithful followers. The mystical Christ has not yet attained to his full growth; and therefore the same is true of the cosmic Christ. Both of these are in the state of being and of becoming; and it is from

77

the prolongation of this process of becoming that all created activity ultimately springs. Christ is the end-point of the evolution, even the *natural* evolution, of all beings; and therefore evolution is holy' (*Hymn of the Universe*, p. 133).

# [4]

## *What does the individual person do?*

THE QUESTION of action always looms large in our minds when we are considering almost any problem. That is natural enough for, if there is nothing we can do about it, then we take quite a different attitude towards the issue. According to our temperament, we either grin and bear it, become bitter about our incapacity to change it, or shrug our shoulders and think no more about it.

When the matter concerns the truth about the world and the part which we can play in the unfolding pattern of events, then the question about action becomes of *vital* interest in the literal sense of that adjective—a matter of life or death. But we need to give more thought than we commonly do to the connection between thought and action. The British are reputed to prefer not to think overmuch about theories and principles, but to concern themselves only with practical affairs. We hear a good deal about British common sense, though I think that less is heard of it in these days than in the past. We talk of the British 'muddling through' and almost regard this attitude to life as a virtue, instead of what it is, a dangerous form of laziness.

In religion this attitude comes out in the frequently stated point of view that it does not matter much what one believes. Afer all everyone is entitled to his own opinions, and what really matters is the sort of person you are and the way in which you behave. There is enough truth in this attitude to make it acceptable on the surface. But, if we probe beneath the surface, we quickly find how very misleading it is.

It is quite clear that beliefs lead to actions in religion, and beliefs which are radically different from one another will produce widely differing standards of behaviour. Those who believe that human action cannot have the slightest effect on the course of the world will adopt a fatalistic attitude, which makes no attempt to influence the course of events. It is quite obvious that social conditions which prevail in certain parts of the world are directly linked to religious beliefs, whether they concern a religious caste structure, sacred cows, or the position of women.

It is important also to observe that, whether or not we actually work out the beliefs and attitudes which underlie action, we cannot in fact adopt any course of action without in some way giving expression to an implied belief. An action may result from one of a number of beliefs and it may be impossible to say which one until investigation has been made. But certain actions, though the exact belief lying behind them may not be clear, do in fact rule out some beliefs and make others credible.

Let us take the simple example of a man who is habitually cruel to animals. We assume that the cruelty does not arise from subnormal intelligence, for in such cases a rational explanation is impossible to find. A man who is habitually cruel to animals shows by that fact that he does not believe that animals are a part of God's creation to which he has any responsibility. He may say that he has never given the matter a moment's thought, but whether he has done so or not, his action is completely incompatible with such a belief as has just been mentioned. By his action he is in fact denying that man has any responsibility towards animals, and is maintaining that he may do as he wishes.

That is a negative conclusion. His action may arise from one of several alternative possibilities of belief. He may think that animals are a danger to him and must be controlled by fear; or he may think that animals do not have any rights and that he is at liberty to behave towards them as he likes; and there are a number of other possibilities of explaining the beliefs which lie behind the actions. The point is that one does not avoid the proclamation of beliefs merely by side-stepping the task of thinking them out. Men's actions imply standards of belief which are reflected in their behaviour.

In the religious field this is also obvious. We have cases which appear fairly often in the newspapers recounting the deaths of children who have not been allowed to have the blood transfusions which they need because their parents belong to the body called Jehovah's Witnesses. They have the absurd idea that blood transfusion is forbidden in the Old Testament and that the prohibition applies to them today, ideas which are ridiculous, unchristian, and completely unbiblical. Although it might be a controversial thing to do, it would probably be possible to trace different behaviour patterns arising in different branches of the Christian religion and to relate them to the underlying beliefs which affected them and even produced them.

We have then to remember two things. First that, whether we are conscious of it or not, our beliefs (which may be well worked out and clear, or hardly conscious at all and very dim) govern our actions. The whole attitude which governs our life shows itself in the way in which we react to the various situations which we face day by day. That is the first point. The second is the other side of it. Whether we have given thought to the matter or not, other people will judge our beliefs by what they see us do. It is not the least good professing the best and most blameless forms of belief if our behaviour tells a different story.

All this is well known to us, but most of the time we prefer to forget it. 'Practise what you preach' we tell other people. Jesus told his listeners that the tree would be known by its fruits, and by this I suppose he meant that the character of a man and his beliefs is shown in the way he behaves. This is sometimes given a wrong twist. It is taken to mean that it does not matter what sort of person you are, or what you believe, so long as the fruit of good behaviour is to be found. But this is the opposite meaning of what is intended. For what Jesus is saying is that the fruit cannot be right unless the tree is right, namely the character and beliefs of the man, the quality of his personality. And we know in our own garden that, if the tree does not produce the right sort of fruit. we have to give our attention to the root of the plant, its nourishment, the condition of its growth—all those things which will make the plant itself healthy, for when that is achieved the fruit will follow. And the fruit will not only look good, it will also taste good and have all the qualities for which it is grown.

These facts about the integral connection between belief and action, character and behaviour are amply borne out by detailed consideration of what makes us come to one decision rather than to another. If we are faced with a problem of acting, of choosing one of a number of courses, we can list the important elements in our decision under various heads. The situation needs first to be analysed and diagnosed. We must not allow ourselves to be governed by what may turn out to be a superficial assessment of the facts which are before us. We may not always be able to do this satisfactorily, but it would be a stupid thing in any serious matter not to try to acquire all the relevant information and to sift it into what is and what is not important.

There we find another aspect, the judgement of what is important and what is not. Importance in any problem depends on the aim or purpose which we have in view. And our aim and purpose depends on what we ourselves think it worth while to try to achieve. This brings us right back to the central influence of our belief. Our belief about ourselves, about the world, about God, governs the order of priorities which we give to the various alternative choices with which we are faced.

If we try to derive our standards from the New Testament, our order of values will be different from those who do not do so. Perhaps this surprises you, but it should not come as any surprise to find this is the case.

'Well,' you may say, 'most of my friends who are not Christians have the same kind of values as I have: in practice I just do not find that my values are different because I am a Christian.'

There are two possible explanations of such a state of affairs if that is an accurate statement. It may be that your friends have adopted Christian values as a result of unconsciously breathing in the air of an environment of which much was Christian. If so, we may be glad. And, parallel to this, are those who have been unable to accept the Christian faith because of some misunderstanding, possibly due to the failure or shortcomings of us or other Christians. Yet they may still be pursuing the truth and finding it in ways which we do not know. Here too we must learn to be thankful for this good, even without those helps which we have through the Church and through our deeper knowledge of God's Word.

But there may be a much less happy explanation. Perhaps we have adjusted ourselves so well and efficiently to the standards of this world that we have to all intents and purposes abandoned those of the New Testament. It is at this point that there is constant need for re-examination and rechecking of our own inner attitudes. We must frankly face the fact that a vast number of nominal Christians do not in their hearts accept, or in their lives put into practice, the values and standards which they see in the life of Jesus. A very simple example which will hit all of us is the failure of Christians to accept sacrifice readily in order to witness to love, instead of our usual practice of insisting on our rights, and spending much of our time and ingenuity in justifying ourselves and our points of view to other people.

Our values are derived from what we believe to be important, which in turn are directly linked to our convictions about the world and our place in it: this again is dependent on what we think about God. Of course, it is not enough just to show these links, though we must see their importance. In real life there is unfortunately a gap—several gaps—between what we believe in our hearts and what we practise in our daily lives. We really do believe in God and in the revelation of his love in Jesus, but our own lives do not come anywhere near to showing that belief in the way we behave and conduct our affairs. What is the remedy for this?

It is perhaps worth saying first that we should not be in too much of a hurry. This, I see, is a very dangerous statement to make, but, as it is true, it has to be made. We must not expect to be suddenly quite free from all the faults with which we know ourselves to be plagued. Life does not work like that, as we can see from the New Testament if we care to look, and as we know from our everyday experience. Peter and Paul did not suddenly become free of all sin and faults. We know the story of Peter's threefold denial: we can read of the rather stupid and unnecessary quarrel which Paul had with Barnabas about whether to take John Mark with them (Acts 15:39). The dispute was so sharp that they parted company. And we know in ourselves and others that past bad habits and present weaknesses show themselves in ways which we regret but still find recurring.

We must not lose heart. God has given us a lifetime in which to grow into his love. One mistake which we must take particular care to avoid is to set up some static idea of perfection at which we are to aim, and

85

imagine that when we eventually climb to that plateau we shall have arrived—with great sighs of relief. Many of us do, I believe, unconsciously have some such picture. But it is unconnected with the truth. Perfection is not static but a dynamic relation with God: it is something which is never ending, for it is a relationship of love which can never be completely exhausted and fully explored. It is therefore a growing thing. If we want to put it into terms of action, we might say that perfection is relative to our own position at any one time, and that it represents the maximum response to the love of God of which we are capable in any particular situation.

Perfection therefore is a moving and dynamic concept: it is something which is experienced in the struggle, something which is wrought in the difficulty of learning obedience to the demands of God's love. That is why we must not lose heart or expect some imaginary kind of rest or achievement, measured by external standards. But of course if we are merely content to sit still and make no effort to respond to the demands which come to us through life, then we find spiritual death, for there is no movement in which we can be formed or find our growth in the love of God.

Such language makes no sense unless at the back of everything there is vision. That is the really important vision which sees a little, however, imperfectly, into the nature of things. It has glimpsed the truth about the world, about men, about ourselves, and seen these things in the light of God's truth. Once having had this glimpse, we can never again abandon it without giving up what we instinctively know to be the most important thing in life. It is a sight that has come from hearing the Word of God.

Vision then is needed. But it has to be renewed and revitalised all the time. One way in which this is done is by putting it into practice in our lives, that is by relating it to the things we have to do and the people we have to meet every day. This can only be done by each person in his or her own circumstances. But so that it does not sound entirely abstract we might ask ourselves such questions as: How is the love of God in my heart to show itself in relation to that beastly snivelling office boy, or to that girl who seems to have no morals at all and is constantly upsetting things? But perhaps even more telling is to ask how it affects what we do and say to and about that man or woman whom in our heart we find so distasteful and unpleasant. Our vision has to be kept clear if it is to stand up to these tests.

But even in the best circumstances we are going to have failures. We need persistence, which will keep on going, keep on getting up after we have fallen down, keep on coming back when we have strayed. This is perhaps the most important of the practical virtues of the Christian life. It depends on our vision, but also on our disciplining of ourselves. It is no good thinking that we can jog along without taking ourselves in hand. We are all subject to discipline whether we like it or not. In order to earn our daily living we have to attend our offices, or shops, or factories, whether we feel happy to do so or whether we would rather be elsewhere. This is a discipline which gives a framework to our life. The discipline which we need from a Christian point of view is not mortification, not engaging in all kinds of unpleasant things because we think it is a heroic sort of sanctity. True Christian character has nothing to do with such practices.

Our discipline must be a rule of life, aimed at making sure that the minimum elements of Christian life are secured to us, for without them we cannot possibly bring into the whole of our lives the love of God, which the Christian message is alone concerned with. Here again there is no rule which applies to everyone. Housewives have one set of problems each of which has to be solved in its own way. Mothers with young children at home, mothers whose children are at boarding schools, mothers with teenage children living at home, all have different difficulties and different opportunities. So it is with men and women at office, factory, or shop. But each should have a rule aimed at keeping the vision of God alive, and of intensifying the insights into the meaning of life and the way in which it can become impregnated with the Spirit of God.

Each of us must make his or her own rule. And again let me add a warning. It should be a minimum rule, something which can normally be kept without too much strain. Extra things can be done when these are possible, but the rule should not make life more difficult all round. I am constantly surprised at how many people use a rule of life to make more sins for themselves, as if we had not enough already! A rule is a guide to help us to come back again and again to the things which really matter, so that we do not just chuck them up when we feel disinclined to pursue them.

What should the rule cover? We leave out the matter of going to church, which will certainly be part of the regular pattern of the life of every person who is seriously trying to explore and follow the Christian way. The rule should cover regular reading and pondering on the New Testament, regular times of prayer and silence, and other things such as stewardship of money, and spare time, if any. We shall not deal much with the detail of prayer but there are some points which may be made about it. You may notice that the expression used was 'times of prayer and silence': these times should include what we normally think of as 'prayers', in particular intercession for those people who we know to be in need of them. But it is vital that there should also be a time of 'waiting upon God', when we are mainly concerned not with prayerful activity, but with opening ourselves to God, exposing ourselves to him—a kind of spiritual sun-bathing, in which we are alert for the word of God to us, and are not shutting our ears because we are talking so much ourselves. We often talk so loudly that we can't hear anything.

Let us note that prayer is a kind of learning to love, being with God in order to love him more. It is certainly not to be confined to special times of silence and apartness, but those times are needed for the purpose of making our whole lives prayerful. We are sometimes told nowadays that prayer is meeting people, or that it is some kind of personal confrontation with others, or that it is in fact anything *except* what has usually been considered to be prayer, namely spending time quietly in the presence of God in the absence of our normal activities.

We must be clear that prayer which is confined to such times, that is prayer which is kept in a little compartment of withdrawal, is in no sense true prayer in the Christian meaning of the word. Prayer has to spread out all through our lives. It is like the love of husband and wife. That love spreads all through their lives, informing all their actions and attitudes, underlying even the most trivial and mundane of tasks. But it needs to be nurtured in special moments of intimacy and silence, and without them it tends to lose its depth.

Prayer needs its times of silence and apartness just in order to maintain its depth throughout the rest of our lives. I have never known of anyone who lived a life of prayer who did not have times of special prayer. All the teachers throughout the ages speak of the need for these special times. But let us be clear that the object of prayer is not withdrawal from life but deeper engagement in it. As a matter of common experience it is not possible to deepen our understanding of God's plan and man's needs without opening ourselves to him in prayer.

The point was put well some years ago by J. N. Figgis: 'Prayer is possible at any time, but the man who prays when he is cleaning his boots is always likely to be the man who has set apart times to keep up the habit.' This applies to the *habit* of prayer, but it is even more applicable to the *depth* of prayer, so that we can both sense and meet the needs of others, and offer our own activities as a sacrifice in the cause of the love of God.

Prayer is the means by which God teaches us to love, and, as he teaches us love, he gives us the vision of the inner nature of things as he himself is in them and is upholding them. A great writer many centuries ago once put this in a Latin epigram: *Ubi amor ibi oculus* —'where love is, there is the power to see' (Richard of St Victor). Both go together, and together they form the inner life of the whole of Christianity and of those who try to follow Christ.

We ought not to be afraid of the word 'mysticism'

in this connection. We should put out of our minds the idea that mysticism means seeing visions, or being elevated from the floor, or being carried away in ecstasies, and see what it really is, learning to make contact with the mysteries of God, learning to contemplate. In its broader and proper sense it is another name for prayer, the mystic life is the life of prayer for every Christian, and we are all mystics. This information may frighten or please, but it is certainly true. The mystic life is the life of vision by which we learn to see within the outer shell to the inner reality, and to perceive what is the character of the life which moves within the whole universe.

It is sometimes said that mysticism or contemplation is to be found in all the great religions, and in a sense this is true. But we can only speak of them all in the same way by pretending that their differences are unimportant, whereas in fact the differences between Eastern and Christian mysticism are great. In saying this, we do not therefore suggest that non Christian mysticism is devoid of insights into truth. Far from it: God has been and is known in some degree by all those who seek after him. But Christian mysticism is in many ways the opposite of that which is most common in the East. Whereas one is world denying, Christian contemplation is world affirming, though there have been some Christians who have failed to understand this fact. Indeed we might sum up this difference in words which we have already used: false mysticism is withdrawal and disengagement from the world; true mysticism, Christian prayer, is engagement with the world at a deeper and deeper level.

It is through reading the New Testament and to a lesser extent the Old, through our prayers, through our

91

waiting upon God, that our love in our prayer is nourished. It is then expressed and also nourished through our contacts with other people in the world, so that practice of prayer in special times and the expression of it in daily life act and interact on one another to bring forward our growth in love and vision.

And in our prayer we grapple with evil. There are many kinds of evil in the world, much of which is outside our personal influence in any direct way. But evil comes to a point in persons, and first of all in our own personalities. Evil begins to be defeated when within our own personalities it is exposed to the light of God. This means a radical readiness to face within ourselves facts which we often try to hide. The prayers at the time of the Reformation and the years succeeding them often used language which seems to put an undue stress on the sinfulness of mankind. The Church of England Prayer Book is a case in point, containing as it does a great many prayers in which we call ourselves miserable sinners and call for mercy in what many today feel to be exaggerated language. Indeed some recent writers have characterized such language as neurotic and even 'un-Christian', as a psychological form of self-flagellation, and other deplorable things.

It is not uncommon for present day writers to consider themselves better balanced than their predecessors and there may be some truth in it. But it strikes me as rather ironic that people should be objecting to this language at the very time when psychological knowledge is in fact revealing to us that we are much worse even than we thought. Indeed we are told that our unconscious is full of ravening wickedness, and that most of our attempts at doing good and our better ideals are nothing more than a cloak to cover the unpleasant features of our hidden personalities. One would therefore have thought that the present would be a time for reviving language about miserable sinners rather than abandoning it!

But no doubt we need to use language which is more realistic to our contemporaries. The writers to whom I refer have the laudable object of persuading us to face the truth about ourselves, and this is an aim which no Christian can do other than encourage. The first way of doing this is to let ourselves be open to the light of God in our prayer when, as we come closer to him, he will show to us the truth about ourselves. This is not a palatable experience, but when it occurs it enables us to offer everything to God, even what is bad and imperfect, and he takes away its power to harm.

Evil in the form of our own sin has to be accepted and offered to God for redemption. This does not mean it has to be approved, but it is a fact, and all facts have to be taken and accepted before they can be transfigured and used. The nature of forgiveness has to be more and more appreciated, and Christians have to work hard to rid themselves of unworthy notions of forgiveness which so often prevent others, as well as themselves, from discovering the depths of the true Gospel.

In all of us there is a tendency to introduce into our relations with God legal categories in some subtle guise. But this is never done without weakening the impact of the Gospel and throwing important matters out of perspective. We do not like, for example, to accept in its full meaning the forgiveness of our sins without any kind of merit on our part. Of course we know that this is the heart of the Gospel and the thing about which we are always rejoicing. But deep within us there is a subtle pride which does not like accepting a gift which is totally unconnected with our own worth. We like to deserve our prize, for that ministers to our self-satisfaction. Whereas on the other hand we do not see why all those others who have not made the efforts which we have made should have the same benefits. In fact we are often, however secretly, like the early labourers in the vineyard, who did not like to see those who had laboured only for one hour getting the same as they did, and so they grumbled and resented it.

We are not as crude as they, but our acceptance of forgiveness is sometimes tainted with the idea that we have earned it by repentance. Nothing of the kind is true. God's forgiveness always precedes our repentance. What we do is to accept it. God's forgiveness is his ever active and present love for those who are sinners: what we have to do is to say 'Yes' to that love. The truth of St Paul's wonderful sentence must come home to us again and again until it sinks into the depths of our personalities, that while we were yet sinners Christ died for us. God loves us as we are, sinners as we are: he doesn't like the sin, but he loves us in our sin, and it is just because of this that the power of his love can draw us out of our sin.

It is impossible for us to say anything really useful to others outside the Christian fold unless we have entered into the inner meaning of God's loving forgiveness, for it is this which changes everything and it is this from which the understanding of God's love for the whole world alone springs. And until this reality has been fully absorbed by us we are unable to face the truth about ourselves, expose the evil within our hearts, and draw from it its sting.

All this is old stuff, it may be said. But it has been overlaid by subtle legalism and wrong attitudes so that we have to strip off the covers again and renew our understanding of it.

When this is done we are at the point where evil can be defeated, and not only defeated but actually made to serve the purposes of God. How can this be when evil is a rebellion against God? It is just because rebellion is the essence of evil that it can be redeemed. Evil in ourselves and in other people, which is where it chiefly matters, is a turning away from God. When it is defeated, this victory is secured by a turning back to God, the *metanoia* of the New Testament. Then the evil may become a stepping stone which can be used to positive effect. Evil is made the very means of redeeming people and the world. Is not this plain enough in the cross?

Teilhard de Chardin in his classical book on the spiritual life, *Le Milieu Divin*, has some good words to say on this point: 'In virtue of his very perfections, God cannot ordain that the elements of a world in the course of growth—or at least of a fallen world in the process of rising again—should avoid shocks and diminishments, even moral ones: *necessarium est ut scandala eveniant*. But God will make it good—He will take his revenge, if one may use the expression—by making evil itself, serve a higher good of his faithful, the very evil which the present state of creation does not allow him to suppress immediately. Like an artist who is able to make use of a fault or an impurity in the stone he is sculpting or the bronze he is casting so as to produce more exquisite lines or a more beautiful tone, God, without sparing us the partial deaths, nor the final death, which form an essential part of our

95

lives, transfigures them by integrating them in a better plan—*provided we lovingly trust in him*. Not only our unavoidable ills but our faults, even our most deliberate ones, can be embraced in that transformation, provided always we repent of them. Not everything is immediately good to those who seek God; but everything is capable of becoming good: *omnia convertuntur in bonum*' (p. 65).

Transfiguration: that is, the use of the outer and obvious parts of our lives to convey an inner reality and meaning within. In the transfiguration of Christ we see the key to his own life and that of the world. George MacLeod of the Iona Community wrote some time ago on this topic. Here are some of his remarks: 'Suppose the material order, as we have argued, is indeed the garment of Christ, the Temple of the Holy Ghost? Suppose the bread and wine, symbols of all creation, is indeed capable of redemption awaiting its Christification? Then what is the Atom but the emergent Body of Christ? It was on the mountain top that Jesus was transfigured. He spoke with Moses and Elijah in the *ruach* (Hebrew for Spirit) world. He also spoke with the disciples in the *ruach* (Hebrew for breath) world, on the mountain top. He was the At One Ment: the key to the spiritual and the material: unifying Love. And His whole *body* glistened, the preview of His resurrection Body. The Feast of the Transfiguration is August 6th. That is the day when we "happened" to drop the bomb at Hiroshima.

'We took His Body and we took His Blood and we enacted a Cosmic Golgotha. We took the Key to Love and we used it for bloody hell.

'Nobody noticed. I am not being cheap about other people. I did not notice it myself. I was celebrating the

96

Feast of the Transfiguration, in a gown and a cassock, a hood, a stole, white bands, saying with the whole Christian Ministry, "This is my Body . . . This is my Blood".

'The while our "Christian civilization", without Church protest, made its assertion of the complete divorce between Spirit and Matter.

'One man noticed. When the word came through to Washington of the dropping of the atom bomb— "Mission successfully accomplished"—Dr Oppenheimer in large degree in our name its architect, was heard to say, "Today, the world has seen Sin".

'Should any reader of this suppose that August 6th, 1945 was Nadir, the lowest point in human disobedience, let us remember the world potential for perpetrating bloody hell ("as the lesser of two evils") is now a million times Hiroshima. It was no pacifist alarmist but the late President Kennedy who was asked how many megatons were needed. He replied, "What we have *on hand* will kill over 300 million people in one hour" (*The Iona Community—Whither Away?*, 1965, p. 12).

The later figures given by Mr MacNamara were worse than that. We need not share all the views of George MacLeod, but this passage rightly brings home to us in a fearsome way the strength of the evil which surrounds us, and in which we are involved in our day. It is this which is making clear to men, one hopes, the stark choice which lies before them—'I have set before you life and death: therefore choose life'. But unless we can help men to see the real meaning of the universe and God's plan for it and in it, they will perhaps choose death.

The vision of the world which Christians must try

to share with every man is the only means by which the evil can be recognized, isolated, and overcome. One reason why there is at present a moral uncertainty even within the Christian Churches, is that Christians have not adjusted themselves to the fact that the advancing frontiers of knowledge and of the power which it brings makes the rigid framework of the past totally out of date so far as morals are concerned. It does not mean that the moral principles of the past are no longer of use: it means that we cannot take nineteenth or eighteenth or tenth or first century application of those principles in the form of rules and apply them as regulations to our position in the middle of the twentieth.

But at the same time the new approach to the meaning of the world, of evolution, of the spiritual value of matter, provides new insights into the principles which must govern our thinking and acting. Let us take an example. The whole moral problem of the control of the birth of babies has been changed by scientific knowledge. Contraceptives make it possible to prevent conception, the pill will probably soon be even more widely used to control ovulation in women. The termination of pregnancies is now much easier and safer than it has ever been in the first months of pregnancy: it is possible that before long this too may be controlled by a pill. In other ways such as multibirth techniques, the determination of sex and so on, possibilities are extending. In this situation phoney reasons for moral or immoral actions just won't do: they will be shown to be phoney.

Many people have for years been telling young people not to indulge in sexual intercourse because they might become pregnant or might get VD or for some reason of a practical kind. These are not moral principles at all, and when it becomes possible to have sexual intercourse without any of these risks, then those who have refrained on these grounds see no further reason to do so. This is what is now happening all over the country. Sexual intercourse is taking place between unmarried couples on a scale never known hitherto, although it has always occurred to a certain extent.

This is not the right occasion to go into the ethics and morals of sex. The only point to be made is that Christians must take a line with regard to morals which makes sure that they consider these moral issues in the light of the insights into truth, spiritual and moral, which we derive from God. The H Bomb is on a world scale a reflection of the situation in our moral life all around us. Christians will only be able to give guidance to themselves and others if they see things clearly in the light of the truth of the love of God and his purpose for the world. This truth tells us that material and physical things only make sense and come to fruition when they are the expression of the deepest things of the Spirit, not the gratification of passion, or of sentimental feelings, but of God's will and intention. And in all our attempts to rethink our moral attitudes and ways of putting things, we must be informed through and through with the compassion of God himself who looks on us and every one of our fellow human beings with infinite love.

In doing this we must cast aside the attitude which has sometimes been found among Christians that the world and material things are in some way contaminated or evil in themselves. We must willingly, no— happily, recognize the contributions of others which help towards God's plan, even though they lack some of the insights which we value. Teilhard tells us what sort of outlook to have: 'Once we have jealously safeguarded our relation to God encountered, if I may dare to use the expression "in His pure state" (that is to say in a state of Being distinct from all the constituents of the world), there is no need to fear that the most trivial or the most absorbing of occupations should force us to depart from Him. To repeat: by virtue of the Creation and still more, of the Incarnation, *nothing* here below is *profane* for those who know how to see. On the contrary, everything is sacred to the men who can distinguish that portion of chosen being which is subject to Christ's drawing power in the process of consummation. Try, with God's help, to perceive the connection—even physical and natural—which binds your labour with the building of the Kingdom of Heaven; try to realize that heaven itself smiles upon you, and, through your works, draws you to itself; then, as you leave church for the noisy street, you will remain with only one feeling, that of continuing to immerse yourself in God' (*Le Milieu Divin*, p. 38).

There is to be no division between what we are doing in our work and what we are doing in our more specifically 'religious' activities. If we think of religion as separate from our work then the sooner we throw such a religion overboard the better, for that is a basically false point of view. We have to get used to the idea that we are being most religious in the right sense of the word when we are immersed in our work, and are trying through it to contribute to the bringing of all things to Christ. It is for this that our so-called 'religious' activities are provided. On the other hand we must never allow ourselves to be so taken up with what we are engaged on in the world that we lose our perspective and our capacity for relating them to God.

God needs our co-operation because he loves us and this co-operation is needed for the full flowering of that love. For the co-operation to grow fully the consciousness of its importance and meaning needs to be extended to all mankind. In the Church we have to nourish and deepen this consciousness. Some men are indeed co-operating in this work without seeing its full implications. We must know them to be on God's side in moving the world towards a new and converging unity of love.

But at the centre stands the cross, and it is the cross which gives ultimate meaning and assurance that all is not in vain. It provides our inner conviction that nothing which is offered to God in simple faith is or can be lost. It bears its fruit in spite of all appearances to the contrary.

Christ is the key to the cosmos. The cross sums up the truths which have been established for ever.

There suffering triumphs. We do not find a satisfying intellectual explanation of suffering and pain. We see the suffering, physical, mental, and spiritual, freely accepted and offered to God, and in that offering we see victory. The cry of triumph which Jesus shouted on the cross 'It has been completed' did not come on Easter morning but at three o'clock on Good Friday afternoon.

On the cross we see that failure wins. There could be no greater failure than that. Everything went: the whole affair collapsed in a sordid and shameful end. But it was the failure that was the measure of the victory.

Nothing is left on the cross as the figure of the dead

101

man is taken down and put into the nearby sepulchre. There isn't *anything* left—there is absolutely nothing. But, miracle of miracles, everything is made out of that nothing. A whole new world is created out of nothing. If that is not the new creation, I don't know what is.